MW00712575

ATLANTA
GUIDEBOOK

*The Definitive Guide
To the South's
Premier City*

Compiled by Candace Springer

LONGSTREET PRESS, INC.
Atlanta, Georgia

Published by
LONGSTREET PRESS, INC.
2150 Newmarket Parkway
Suite 102
Marietta, Georgia 30067

Printed in the United States of America

1st printing, 1991

Library of Congress Catalog Card Number
90-063898

ISBN 0-929264-90-8

This book was printed by Arcata
Graphics Book Group, Kingsport, Tennessee.
The text type was set in Bodoni by
Typo-Repro Service, Inc., Atlanta, Georgia.
Cover design by Jill Dible.

Photo Credits:
Cover photo—Atlanta Chamber of Commerce
pp. 6, 7, 10, 20, 30, 37, 41, 47, 56, 62, 71, 109,
134, 163, 164, 177, 179—Atlanta Chamber of
Commerce; p. 39—The World of Coca-Cola;
p. 51—The Fox Theatre; p. 75—The
Buckhead Diner; p. 82—The Peasant
Restaurants; p. 96—Don Juan's Restaurant;
p. 100—Pano's & Paul's; p. 106—Melear's
Barbecue; p. 114—Blues Harbor; p. 117—
Petrus; p. 121—The Ritz Carlton, Buckhead;
p. 126—Manuel's Tavern; p. 157—Vinings
Jubilee Shopping Center; p. 180—Delta
Airlines

WELCOME TO ATLANTA

Visitors who expect Atlanta to wear an Old South aspect will discover a city which, though respectful of the past, is certainly not enslaved by it. The Old South is captured in the lifelike painting of the Battle of Atlanta at the Cyclorama; it resonates in the battlefields at Kennesaw Mountain; it is rendered in granite on the side of Stone Mountain, and perhaps it is recalled most vividly in the graves of thousands of Confederate soldiers at the Marietta National Cemetery. But Atlanta's vision of the future rescues it from the mire of provincialism. The recent revival of Underground Atlanta pays homage to Atlanta's symbol of the Phoenix rising from the ashes and has helped to broaden Atlanta's appeal to out-of-towners and residents alike.

Architect John Portman's strictly modern structures in downtown Atlanta have been duplicated in other cities. As Atlanta has moved northward, a less rigid, more eclectic style has emerged in the skyscrapers that grace the Midtown area, but Portman's mark on the Atlanta skyline remains indelible and a testament to the city's pioneering spirit.

Transportation probably did a great deal to spare Atlanta from the fate of other southern cities. Founded as a railroad town in the mid-nineteenth century, Atlanta has always been a crossroads. Today it functions as the airline hub of the Sunbelt and is home to Delta Airlines. With its rapid-rail system firmly entrenched and expanding, Atlanta remains a model for many urban areas.

Atlanta's foreign population has burgeoned in recent years, bringing the city's total number of inhabitants to more than 2.5 million. The international complexion of the city has further been enhanced by the selection of Atlanta as the site for the 1996 Summer Olympics. You will notice the impact of different ethnic groups on the variety of eating establishments Elliott Mackle (restaurant critic for the *Atlanta Journal-Constitution*) has chosen for inclusion in the restaurant guide. Eating out can be an adventure when it includes everything from Ethiopian to Japanese cuisine. Shopping, nightlife, and the proliferation of performing and visual arts also reflect this cultural diversity.

First-time visitors invariably comment on the abundance of trees and shrubs in Atlanta. If you are fortunate enough to be here in the month of April, you will be privileged to see the brilliant azaleas accented by snowy and petal-pink dog-woods which turn Atlanta into a veritable fairy-land. A walk through the Fernbank Forest or along the Chattahoochee River will give you a fur-ther appreciation of the natural landscape and an idea of the environment the Native Americans enjoyed here several centuries ago.

To discover the essence of Atlanta is not possible without mention of some of the dreamers, past and present, who have been an integral part of Atlanta's history: Martin Luther King, Jr., who dreamed of civil rights for all; Jimmy Carter, who envisions world peace through diplomacy and negotiation; and Billy Payne, whose dream of Atlanta hosting the 1996 Summer Olympics has become a reality. Each of these people is inex-tricably connected to the heart and soul of this city.

From its native roots as an Indian outpost, to its railroad days, through its antebellum period and Reconstruction, Atlanta has never capitulated to defeat. In this selective guide you can find places to explore the historical significance of this tenacity or you can relish the fact that Atlanta is a cultural and entertainment center of the South and simply enjoy your stay. Whatever your reason for visiting, Atlanta bids you a warm southern welcome. ■

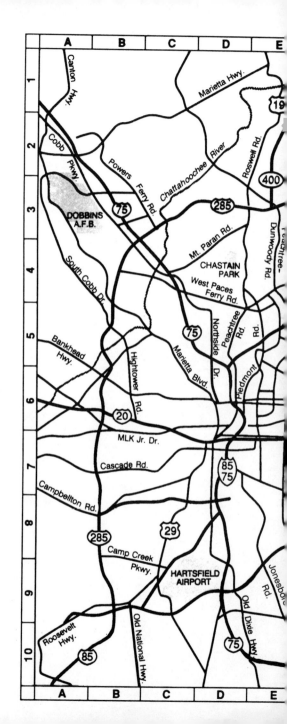

METRO ATLANTA MAP

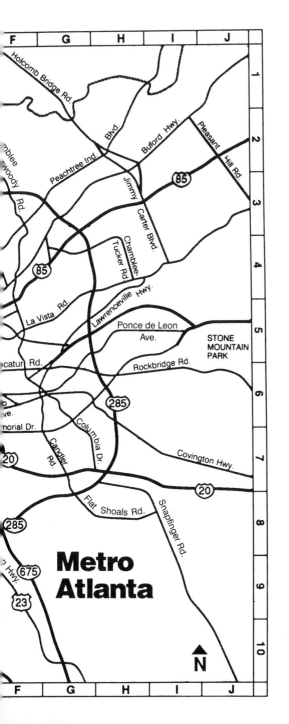

Metro Atlanta

N

THE INDEX

INDEX

ATTRACTIONS

Atlanta offers an enticing variety of things to see and do. The many Civil War sites, museums and exhibits are manna for history buffs, but there's much more to the city than its Confederate connections. The greenery of the city is resplendent in its parks and river walks. The importance of its African-American heritage is kept alive in the Martin Luther King, Jr., Historic District and is re-emphasized in the prestigious black universities and colleges located here. Negotiations and diplomatic efforts at the Carter Center regularly propel Atlanta into international headlines. And activities for children and families are plentiful: from the educational Scitrek to the exhilarating Six Flags Over Georgia. Although this listing is selective, it should provide more than a few busy days for anyone visiting the city.

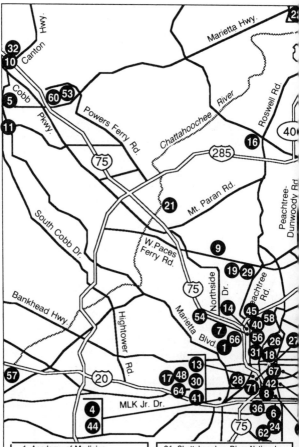

1. Academy of Medicine
2. Bulloch Hall
3. Cabbagetown
4. CNN Center
5. Confederate Cemetery
6. Cyclorama
7. Fox Theatre
8. Georgia State Capitol
9. Governor's Mansion
10. Kennesaw National Battlefield
11. Marietta National Cemetery
12. Oakland Cemetery
13. Peachtree Center
14. Rhodes Hall
15. Stone Mountain Village
16. Williams-Payne House
17. Wren's Nest
18. Atlanta Botanical Garden
19. Atlanta History Center Gardens
20. Cator Woolford Memorial Garden

21. Chattahoochee River National Recreation Area
22. Chattahoochee Nature Center
23. Fernbank Forest and Fernbank Greenhouse and Gardens
24. Grant Park
25. Olmsted Parks
26. Piedmont Park
27. Woodruff Park
28. Atlanta-Fulton Public Library Central Branch
29. Atlanta History Center
30. Atlanta Historical Society Information Center
31. Atlanta Museum
32. Big Shanty Museum
33. Carter Presidential Center
34. DeKalb County Historical Society
35. Emory University Museum of Art and Archaeology

36. Georgia Department of Archives
37. Georgia State Museum of Science and Industry
38. Gwinnett County Museum*
39. Hapeville Depot Museum*
40. High Museum of Art
41. High Museum of Art at Georgia-Pacific Center
42. Johnny Mercer Room
43. Marietta/Cobb Museum of Art*
44. Monetary Museum/Federal Reserve Bank
45. Zachor Holocaust Center
46. Apex
47. Ebenezer Baptist Church
48. The Herndon Home
49. Martin Luther King, Jr. Boyhood Home
50. Martin Luther King, Jr. Center for Nonviolent Social Change
51. Martin Luther King, Jr. National Historic Site

52. Sweet Auburn
53. American Adventures
54. Center for Puppetry Arts
55. Fernbank Science Center
56. Scitrek
57. Six Flags Over Georgia
58. "Spectacles"
59. Stone Mountain Memorial Park
60. White Water
61. Yellow River Game Ranch*
62. Zoo Atlanta
63. Agnes Scott College
64. Atlanta University Complex
65. Emory University
66. Georgia Institute of Technology
67. Georgia State University
68. Kennesaw State College*
69. Mercer University
70. Oglethorpe University
71. Underground Atlanta
*Refer to text for location

HISTORICAL SITES AND POINTS OF INTEREST

❶ Academy of Medicine. 875 West Peachtree St. N.E., 874-3219. Although not particularly old, since it was constructed in 1941, the Academy of Medicine appears on the National Register of Historic Places. Designed in the Neoclassic style by renowned architect Philip Trammell Shutze, it is impressive in its symmetry and decor, and its interior contains paintings and other furnishings of note. Renovated in 1983, the structure is used for meetings, dinners, and receptions. The Archives Room contains historical material of the Medical Association and other medical artifacts. Hours: 8:30 a.m.-5:30 p.m., Monday-Friday.

❷ Bulloch Hall. 180 Bulloch Ave., Roswell, 992-1731. Built in 1840, this superb example of temple-form architecture in the Greek Revival style was the home of Martha "Mittie" Bulloch, mother of Theodore Roosevelt. After Mittie married Theodore Roosevelt, Sr., at Bulloch Hall in 1853, the couple moved to New York City. Rented out by the Bulloch family during the War Between the States, the house was protected from destruction when the French flag was flown over the structure, confusing the Union Army. Now maintained as a cultural center, the home contains Civil War artifacts and Bulloch and Roosevelt family heirlooms. Cost: $3 for adults; $1 for children ages 6-16; $2 for senior citizens. Hours: 11 a.m.-2 p.m., Tuesday-Friday.

❸ Cabbagetown. Near the Martin Luther King MARTA train station and east of Oakland Cemetery off Boulevard S.E., this area is a throwback to a bygone time. Row houses crowded onto narrow streets surround an abandoned cotton mill. The mill, when active, attracted economically depressed workers from Appalachia to Atlanta in the 1880s. The new mill employees and their families, however, brought their mountain traditions, handicrafts, and customs with them. Although the mill eventually died, the mountain customs and crafts survived and continue in this neighborhood still. Stop in at Cabbagetown Pottery at 242 Boulevard (525-6383) for a look at some of the crafts produced by the people of Cabbagetown. Hours: 11 a.m.-5 p.m., weekdays; noon-4 p.m. Saturday.

❹ CNN Studio Tour. 100 Techwood Ave. S.W., 827-2300. Ted Turner's famous Cable News Network and CNN Headline News are quartered in what was formerly known as the Omni International Office Complex. The CNN Studio Tour gives visitors a look at the newsrooms and special exhibits which highlight programs of CNN and other acquisitions of media mogul Ted Turner. Movie buffs will be interested in the MGM exhibit; and for wrestling fans, the display featuring CNN World Championship Wrestling is definitely worth a look. Cost: $5 for adults; $2.50 for youths ages 12-18 and senior citizens 65 and older; free for children under 12. Hours: 45-minute tours run 10 a.m.-5 p.m., Monday-Friday and 10 a.m.-4 p.m., Saturday. Arrangements for the handicapped need to be made in advance.

❺ Confederate Cemetery. Corner of Powder Springs and Goss streets, Marietta. The cemetery was established in 1863 after a Confederate troop train wrecked near Marietta and emergency measures were called for to deal with the bodies of soldiers. The cemetery also contains the bodies of soldiers from the Battle of Kennesaw Mountain. About 3000 soldiers from each of the Southern states in the Civil War are buried here.

6 Cyclorama. 800 Cherokee Ave. S.E., 624-1071. Situated in Grant Park next to Zoo Atlanta, the Cyclorama depicts the Battle of Atlanta in a massive circular painting and diorama (a three-dimensional scene). Viewers are seated in a modern theatre which rotates 360 degrees for a narrated presentation of the picture. The painting was completed in 1886 and presented to the city in 1898 by G. V. Greff. The art work is painted on Belgian linen, measures 42 feet high and weighs 9,334 pounds. Close to the size of a football field, its circumference is 358 feet. The figurines in the diorama range from 17 to 42 inches tall. The Cyclorama also includes a museum where visitors can see actual weapons, uniforms, and articles used by soldiers in battle. The famous locomotive, Texas, which chased down the engine, The General, and caught it south of Chattanooga, is housed here, too. In the bookstore you can find an extensive Civil War collection. Cost: $3.50 for adults; $3 for senior citizens; $2 for children ages 6-12; free for children under 6. Hours: 9:30 a.m.-5:30 p.m., daily. Closes at 4:30 p.m. in the winter months. Tours every thirty minutes. Closed major holidays.

7 Fox Theatre. 660 Peachtree St. Box office: 249-6400; administrative offices: 881-2100. One of Atlanta's landmarks, the Fox, with its Byzantine architecture topped by onion domes and minarets, was threatened by extinction in 1975, but was saved by a fervent community campaign. This splendid structure, with its amazing acoustics and its dazzling interior, resembles a canopied Middle-Eastern courtyard with a vista of a cloud-filled, star-studded night sky. Since the Fox opened its doors on Christmas Day in 1929 as a Shriners' hall and movie theatre, it has weathered a rocky career. In 1932 its doors were closed for three years due to financial problems, but when it reopened, it did so with style, adding live performances (including the Metropolitan Opera) and orchestras which played for the dancing set in the Egyptian Ballroom. After its closing in 1975, it wasn't reopened again until 1979. Since then, however, the live performances and summer film festival have kept its 5000 seats full. The Fox contains one of the largest Moller organs in the world. To listen to the sounds of this mighty organ beneath the twinkling stars and drifting clouds of an Arabian night is an experience not to be missed. Cost: $3 for adults; $1 for students and senior citizens; group rates available. Tours at 10 a.m., Monday and Thursday; 10 a.m. and 11:30 a.m., Saturday. No tours in January and February.

8 Georgia State Capitol. Capitol Square S.W., 656-2844. In addition to its role as the law-making assembly of the state, Georgia's State Capitol is full of exhibits, statues, and paintings. Visitors will be asked to sign in with a security guard at either of two entrances. Guided tours are offered on the hour (except noon), or guests can observe the House and Senate while they are in session. Special tours for the sight- or hearing-impaired can be arranged by calling 656-2844. Of special note is the gold-leaf of the dome, mined in the north Georgia town of Dahlonega. The Georgia State Museum of Science and Industry is located on the first and fourth floors of the capitol. Here visitors can view exhibits depicting the natural history of Georgia, including many Indian artifacts dating back 2500 years. Relics of the War Between the States, the Spanish-American War and World War I are on the first floor. Tours 10 a.m.-2 p.m., Monday-Friday. Open to the public 10 a.m.-2 p.m. on Saturday and 1-3 p.m. Sunday.

9 Governor's Mansion. 391 Paces Ferry Road N.W., 261-1776. Seven rooms are open to visitors including the library, state dining room, state drawing room, family living room, family dining room, guest bedroom, and circular hallway. A fine collection of nineteenth-century furnishings, paintings, and porcelains in the neoclassical style grace the mansion. The collection of Federal period furniture is considered one of the finest in the United States. The most valuable item in the mansion is a nineteenth-century porcelain vase in the circular hallway with a portrait medallion of Benjamin Franklin. Bibliophiles will find the collection of signed and first editions by Georgia authors of interest in the library. Tours 10-11:30 a.m., Tuesday-Thursday.

10 Kennesaw National Battlefield. Junction of Old U.S. 41 and Old Stilesboro Rd., Marietta, 427-4686. The 3000-acre park is listed on the National Register of Historic Places, and the battlefield has been preserved to commemorate the Battle of Kennesaw Mountain in 1864 as part of the Atlanta Campaign. The battle took place between Sherman's 100,000 Union soldiers and 65,000 Confederate troops under the command of General Joseph E. Johnston. The park features 17 miles of walking trails, numerous historic markers, and picnic areas. Hours daily: 8:30 a.m.-5:00 p.m. for the visitors' center; 8:30 a.m.-5:30 p.m. for the mountain road; and 8:30 a.m.-6 p.m. for the parking lot.

11 Marietta National Cemetery. Washington Ave. and Cole St., Marietta, 428-5631. The cemetery, which was established in 1866, is the final resting ground for 10,000 Union soldiers, 3000 of whom are unknown. The cemetery covers 23 acres and is primarily a burial spot for soldiers of wars since the War Between the States, although a few interments date from the Revolutionary War and the Indian Wars. Hours: 8 a.m.-5 p.m., daily.

12 Oakland Cemetery. 248 Oakland Ave. S.E., 577-8163. Oakland, Atlanta's first cemetery, was established in 1850 on 88 acres east of downtown. Many of Atlanta's pioneers and notable citizens are buried here, including author Margaret Mitchell, golfer Bobby Jones, five Confederate generals, six governors of Georgia, and 23 mayors of Atlanta. Genealogical research records are housed here, too. Hours: visitors' center open 9 a.m.-5 p.m. Monday-Friday. Group tours available weekdays through Historic Oakland Cemetery Inc., weekends through the Atlanta Preservation Center (522-4345).

13 Peachtree Center. 231 Peachtree St. N.E., 659-0800. Designed by John Portman, this modern complex of office towers is connected by skyway bridges to several of the major downtown hotels. Peachtree Center contains a shopping mall and a fast food court frequented by business people and tourists alike.

14 Rhodes Hall. 1516 Peachtree St. N.E., 881-9980. An imposing granite structure just north of midtown, Rhodes Hall is a superb example of the Romanesque Revival style. Completed in 1904 for furniture magnate A. G. Rhodes, it originally sat on 150 acres of land. At Rhodes' death in 1928, the house was deeded to the state for educational and historic purposes. From 1930 to 1965, the State Archives were housed here. Currently the building serves as the headquarters for the Georgia Trust for Historic Preservation. The interior reflects the elegance and ornamental grace of the Victorian era. Cost: $2 for adults; $.50 for children. Tours 11 a.m.-4 p.m., Monday-Friday.

15 Stone Mountain Village. From downtown take I-85 north to I-285 east; take Exit 30-B, Highway 78; follow signs to Stone Mountain Village; city hall, 498-8985. Established in 1847, the town of Stone Mountain looks very much like it did 100 years ago. Craft shops and stores abound in the quaint village along Main Street. Stone Mountain Craftsmen's Guild Handbag Factory Store produces fine leather work. If you are interested in the past, you might want to stop in at Stone Mountain Relics, specializing in Indian and Civil War memorabilia. Around the corner you can fill up on a homestyle lunch or dinner at the Old Post Office Country Buffet. Stone Mountain Village is accessible by the New Georgia Railroad from downtown, making a nice day trip.

16 Williams-Payne House. 6075 Sandy Springs Circle (between Hammond Cir. and Mount Vernon Hwy., outside I-285), 851-9111. The Williams-Payne house, a clapboard farmhouse more than a century old, was recently moved to the Sandy Springs Historic Site. The farmhouse, originally located on Mount Vernon Rd., was owned by Jerome Williams for fifty years. For the next fifty years it belonged to the Payne family, and many of the antiques which furnish the house today belonged to Marie Payne. Sandy Springs is an unincorporated community in Atlanta which derives its name from the springs which bubbled up through white sands in the area. The springs may be viewed on this site as well. Cost: $2 for adults; $1 for children 12 and older, students and senior citizens. Hours: 10 a.m.-4 p.m., Monday and Wednesday.

17 Wren's Nest. 1050 Gordon St. S.W., 753-8535. Standing in the midst of Atlanta's oldest neighborhood is the home of Joel Chandler Harris, best known for his Uncle Remus characters and the stories *Br'er Rabbit* and *Br'er Fox*. The house dates from the 1870s and was purchased by the Harris family in 1883. Nine rooms are open to the public, featuring original furnishings, photographs, and memorabilia of the family. A slide-show presentation describes the life, times, and works of the author. In the summer months, a storyteller performs three times a day, Tuesdays through Thursdays. Cost: $3 for adults; $2 for teens and senior citizens; $1 for children 4-12. Hours: 10 a.m.-4 p.m., Tuesday-Saturday and 1-4 p.m., Sunday. Call for group rate information. Last tour of the day at 4 p.m.

GARDENS AND PARKS

18 Atlanta Botanical Garden. 1345 Piedmont Ave. N.E., 876-5858. Located in a corner of Piedmont Park, the Atlanta Botanical Garden has grown from a series of small, formal outdoor garden plots to a nationally recognized garden spot in recent years. Here you can linger in a restful Japanese garden, lunch near the splendid rose garden, enjoy the odors in the scent garden, or wander through the herb and vegetable gardens. With the addition of the Dorothy Chapman Fuqua Conservatory, 16,000 square feet of indoor growing space have allowed cultivation of tropical, desert and endangered species. The garden also has nature trails throughout a 15-acre hardwood forest. Each Sunday a documentary film on Piedmont Park is shown in the garden's library and a puppet show is presented for children. The gift shop includes a wide assortment of gardening gifts and accesories. Cost: $4.50 for adults; $2.25 for senior citizens, students and children 6-12; free for children under 6. Hours: 9 a.m.-6 p.m., Tuesday-Saturday; noon-6 p.m., Sunday. Closed on Monday.

19 Atlanta History Center Gardens. 3101 Andrews Dr. N.W., 261-1837. Although these gardens are a part of the Atlanta History Center, they are worth special mention because of the variety of plants represented in this beautiful 32-acre tract. Native and Asian species are designated along the Swan Woods Trail, culminating in the Garden For Peace with its Soviet Peace Tree Sculpture. The Mary Howard Gilbert Memorial Quarry Garden features native wildflowers and connects the Tullie Smith House with McElreath Hall. The Frank A. Smith Memorial Rhododendron Garden and the Sims Garden with its Asian-American flora exemplify contemporary trends in gardens. See **ATTRACTIONS, Museums and Libraries** for costs and hours.

20 Cator Woolford Memorial Garden. 1815 Ponce de Leon Ave. N.E., 377-3836. This forty-year-old sunken garden near the Olmsted Parks on Ponce de Leon Ave. is a remnant of the once gracious estate on this land. Now a part of the Cerebral-Palsy Center, these lovely gardens are maintained by the Fernbank Science Center and provide an outdoor recreation area for the patients as well as the general public. Particularly spectacular when the azaleas and dogwoods are in bloom in the early spring, these gardens are a welcome respite from the busy thoroughfare nearby. Open daylight hours, daily.

21 Chattahoochee River National Recreation Area. A series of park lands along the Chattahoochee River, this National Recreation Area occupies a 48-mile stretch along the water. You can take advantage of a number of recreational activities (rafting, kayaking, canoeing, fishing, hiking, or biking, for instance); or you can experience the beautiful sights and sounds of the river environment, as the Creek and Cherokee Indians did 150 years ago. Call 394-8335 for locations and information about the numerous trails.

㉒ Chattahoochee Nature Center. 9135 Willeo Road, Roswell, 992-2055. This environmental education facility is a perfect place for bird watching, taking nature walks, and learning about the flora and fauna indigenous to Georgia. Situated near the Chattahoochee River, the center features wildlife exhibits, an observation tower, and guided nature hikes. The book-and-gift store sells items related to natural science. Hours: 9 a.m.-5 p.m., daily.

㉓ Fernbank Forest and Fernbank Greenhouse and Gardens. Fernbank Forest is located at 156 Heaton Park Dr., 378-4311. Adjacent to Fernbank Science Center, Fernbank Forest was the home of the Creek Indians until 1821. The land remained relatively undisturbed until it was placed under government protection in 1939, so it provides a rare look at a fairly pristine forest in a city environment. Fernbank Greenhouse and Gardens are located at 120 Briarcliff Rd. Visitors are invited to view and even touch the plants cultivated in the greenhouse. The Botanical Garden includes an herb garden, a rose garden and a demonstration rose garden. Both the Forest and the Greenhouse and Gardens are free to visitors. Hours: Forest open 2-5 p.m., Sunday-Friday; 10 a.m.-5 p.m., Saturday. Greenhouse and Gardens open 1-5 p.m on Sunday only.

㉔ Grant Park. The parcel of land which is now Grant Park was named in honor of its donor, Colonel L. P. Grant, who gave 100 acres of his land to the city of Atlanta in 1883 to be used as a city park. Additional acreage was added to the original plot in 1890. See **Cyclorama** in **ATTRACTIONS, Historical Sites and Points of Interest;** and **Zoo Atlanta** in **ATTRACTIONS, Family and Children's Activities.** Also see **Water Sports** in **RECREATION.**

㉕ Olmsted Parks. Ponce de Leon Ave. N.E. Frederick Law Olmsted, commonly known as the father of landscape architecture and famous for his design of New York's Central City Park, first came to Atlanta in 1890. During this visit he laid the initial plans for Piedmont Park and the Druid Hills neighborhood. In Atlanta, Olmsted is best remembered for the two-mile strip of park area bordering Ponce de Leon Avenue that is a favorite of joggers, children, and those seeking some tranquility from noise and traffic. These parks also provide a welcome sight of greenery to commuters on the heavily traveled east-west city route.

㉖ Piedmont Park. Piedmont Ave. and 14th St. N.E., 658-7406. This 185-acre public park was also designed by Frederick Law Olmsted (see Olmsted Parks above). The city park was created following the Cotton States and International Exposition held in Atlanta in 1895. After the buildings from the lengthy and impressive exhibition were dismantled, the park with its lake and pavilion, wooded walks, and wide grassy expanses became a popular retreat in the midst of a growing city. Piedmont Park plays host to annual events such as the Piedmont Arts Festival and the Dogwood Festival, and it furnishes the finish line for the Peachtree Road Race. See **RECREATION** and **Atlanta Botanical Garden** (above) for additional park activities.

㉗ Woodruff Park. Named after Coca-Cola magnate Robert W. Woodruff, this downtown park is probably Atlanta's closest thing to Hyde Park. Occupying several blocks of open expanse amidst modern skyscrapers and vestiges of old Atlanta architecture, the park bustles with downtown life: business and student lunches, activists and protesters, and street entertainment.

LIBRARIES AND MUSEUMS

28 Atlanta-Fulton Public Library. One Margaret Mitchell Square, 730-1700. The austere Bauhaus design of the library may make the building appear a bit formidable, but inside you will find that the classics are still available, the librarians are most helpful, and the library is user-friendly. Personal computers have replaced the card catalog as a way to access material and are ready with easy-to-follow directions for all patrons to try. Be sure to visit Special Collections which houses Margaret Mitchell's early drafts of *Gone With The Wind.* Hours: 9 a.m.-6 p.m., Monday and Friday; 9 a.m.-8 p.m., Tuesday-Thursday; 10 a.m.-6 p.m., Saturday; 2-6 p.m. Sunday. Branch hours differ.

29 Atlanta History Center. 3101 Andrews Dr. N.W., 261-1837. Discover the unique quality of Atlanta's past and explore the varied aspects of its history at the Atlanta History Center. In McElreath Hall the visitor will find the permanent exhibits: Atlanta and the War, 1861-1865; and Atlanta Resurgens, which tells the story of Atlanta from Reconstruction to the present. There are changing exhibits, too, which focus on period costumes, furnishings, architecture, etc. The library and archives of the Atlanta Historical Society (which are open to the public) and The Cherokee Garden Library, which houses a special collection of gardening books, are also located in McElreath Hall. The Swan House, a 1928 Anglo-

Palladian mansion once owned by Edward and
Emily Inman and designed by noted neoclassical
architect Philip Trammell Shutze, is on the
grounds of the Atlanta History Center. On a tour
of the house you will see how its name is derived
from the recurrence of the swan motif in the
architectural detail. Period furnishings and the
Philip Trammel Shutze Collection of Decorative
Arts are highlights of the interior. Don't miss the
Victorian playhouse in the lovely gardens surrounding the house. The former garage and ser-
vants' quarters have been transformed into the
Swan Coach House Restaurant. The restaurant,
gift shop and art gallery are run by the Forward
Arts Foundation. The Tullie Smith Farm, also
located on the grounds of the Atlanta History
Center, stands in stark contrast to the elegant
Swan House. Built about 1840, it is a prime example of a Georgia pioneer farm. Visitors can tour
the house, outbuildings and adjoining gardens,
and when weather permits, there are demonstrations of hearth cooking. Cost: $6 for adults; $4.50
for students and senior citizens 65 and older; $3
for children 6-17; Free for children under 6.
Admission includes entrance to entire complex.
Hours: 9 a.m.-5:30 p.m., Monday-Saturday;
noon-5 p.m on Sunday. Closed major holidays.
Guided tours 9:30 a.m.-4:30 p.m., Monday-
Saturday; 12:30-4:30 p.m. on Sunday.

**30 Atlanta Historical Society Information
Center.** 140 Peachtree St., 238-0655. Located in
the restored 1911 Hillyer Building downtown, this
branch of the Atlanta History Center's main location in Buckhead enables visitors to find out
about activities in Atlanta which are of historical
interest. Changing exhibits and videos on Atlanta
history provide the visitor with a wealth of information on the city. A museum shop features memorabilia of Atlanta and the South. Hours: 10
a.m.-6 p.m., Monday-Saturday.

31 Atlanta Museum. 537 Peachtree St. N.E.,
872-8233. The Atlanta Museum is located in the
Rufus M. Rose House (the family of Four Rose
Liquor fame). Built in 1900, the house is listed on

the National Register of Historic Places. Both the interior and the exterior of the house remain relatively unchanged and are fine examples of Victorian architecture. History enthusiasts will be fascinated with the objects and artifacts found inside: items chronicling Atlanta's railroad days, furniture from the apartment where Margaret Mitchell wrote *Gone With The Wind*, an original model of the cotton gin which was found in the shop used by Eli Whitney at Washington, Georgia, and Davy Crockett's rifle. Civil war weapons, a World War I cannon, and articles that belonged to Franklin Roosevelt and Adolph Hitler (including clothing, silver flatware, and a bronze bust of Hitler from his Munich home) are on display here, too. A Japanese Zero airplane and a piece of the rope used to hang the Japanese warlord Tojo will be of interest to WWII buffs. Cost: $3 for adults; $1.50 for children; $2.50 for senior citizens. Hours: 10 a.m.-5 p.m., Monday-Friday; Saturday and Sunday by appointment.

32 Big Shanty Museum. 2829 Cherokee St., Kennesaw, 427-2117. See The General, the famous Civil War locomotive chronicled in a popular movie. In 1862 the train was stolen by a Union force known as Andrews' Raiders. Thanks to the efforts of the train's conductor and his group of stalwart Confederates, The General was hotly pursued and subsequently recovered. The engine enjoyed a long career which included its conversion from steam to coal and eventually to oil. For years the locomotive remained in Chattanooga where the L&N Railroad kept it on display, but in 1972 (one hundred years to the day after it was stolen), it was returned to its original home of Kennesaw (formerly known as Big Shanty). Housed in the museum are the engine, various displays and a narrated slide film describing the raid. Cost: $2.50 for adults; $1 for children under 7; $2 for senior citizens 65 and older. Hours: 9:30 a.m.-5:30 p.m. Monday-Saturday; noon-5:30 p.m. Sunday. Closed major holidays. Winter hours: noon-5:30 p.m. daily.

㉝ Carter Presidential Center. One Copenhill Ave. N.E., 331-3942. The Carter Presidential Center sits on 30 acres in the intown neighborhood of Inman Park. The Museum focuses on life in the White House, as well as on important issues and events of the twentieth century. Visitors may enjoy seeing the various gifts bestowed on President Carter during his term of office and an interactive video exhibit allows visitors to pose questions to President Carter. The grounds of the center also contain the Task Force for Child Survival, the offices of Global 2000 (a project dedicated to Third World food problems), the Carter Center of Emory University, which supplies a forum for solving various world problems, and a research facility containing 26 million pages of material from the Carter administration. The beautifully landscaped grounds feature a Japanese waterfall and ample room to stroll and ruminate. Cost: $2.50 for adults; $1.50 for senior citizens 55 and older; free for children under 16. Hours: 9 a.m.-4:45 p.m. Monday-Saturday; noon-4:45 p.m. Sunday. Closed major holidays.

㉞ DeKalb County Historical Society. Old Courthouse on the Square, Decatur, 373-1088. Civil war memorabilia and exhibits pertaining to Indians, pioneer life, and history in the county are on view. Appointments may be made to tour the nearby historical complex with its 1840 home and two log cabins. Free admission. Hours: 9 a.m.-4 p.m. Monday-Friday.

㉟ Emory University Museum of Art and Archaeology. Michael C. Carlos Hall, Main Quadrangle, near the intersection of North Decatur and Oxford roads, 727-7522. This intimate little architectural gem, designed by famed post-modernist Michael Graves, offers the only permanent exhibitions of antiquities in the city. It also features temporary exhibits that run the gamut from ancient to contemporary art. Hours: 11 a.m.-4:30 p.m. Tuesday-Saturday.

36 Georgia Department of Archives. 330
Capitol Ave. S.E., 656-2350. Created in 1918, the
Georgia Department of Archives and History is a
division of the Office of the Secretary of State.
The archives provide a place for significant
records of Georgia history to be kept and are a
treasure trove for those interested in genealogy or
history. County courthouse records, land records,
and an extensive photo collection are available for
perusal. Non-governmental documents include
family letters and papers and materials from
social organizations and churches dating as far
back as the 1700s. Hours: 8 a.m.-4:15 p.m.
Monday-Friday and 9:30 a.m.-3:15 p.m. Saturday.
Closed on state holidays and the Saturday in con-
junction with these.

**37 Georgia State Museum of Science and
Industry.** See **Georgia State Capitol** in
Historical Sites and Points of Interest.

38 Gwinnett County Museum. 455 Perry St.,
Lawrenceville, 822-5178. The museum contains
collections of early educational material, including
furniture, books, photographs, clothing, and toys.
Hours: 10 a.m.-noon and 1-3 p.m. Monday-Friday.
Free admission.

39 Hapeville Depot Museum. 620 S. Central
Ave., Hapeville, 669-2175. Exhibits in this transportation museum feature early air and rail travel
in Atlanta. There is also an operating model railroad. Free admission. Hours: 11 a.m.-3 p.m.
Tuesday-Friday; 1-4 p.m. Sunday.

40 High Museum of Art. 1280 Peachtree St.
N.E., 898-9532. Housed in an award-winning
building designed by Richard Meier, the High is
Atlanta's largest museum and the center of the art
community. It is a generalist institution with a
schedule that attempts to cover all the bases. Its
permanent collection boasts depth in decorative
arts, nineteenth-century American painting, and
photography. Cost: $4 for adults; $1 for children
6-17; free for children under 5; and free to the
general public after 1 p.m. Thursdays. Hours: 10

a.m.-5 p.m. Tuesday-Saturday; noon-5 p.m.
Sunday.

**㊶ High Museum of Art at Georgia-Pacific
Center.** 133 Peachtree St. N.E., 577-6940. This
elegant little downtown museum, winner of a prestigious American Institute of Architects award, is
run by the High, and its offerings mirror the generalist approach evident in the big building up the
street. Two temporary shows usually run concur-
rently, along with a small exhibition of contemporary glass. Free admission. Hours: 11 a.m.-5 p.m.
Monday-Friday.

㊷ Johnny Mercer Room. Special Collections
Department, Pullen Library, Georgia State University, 100 Decatur St. S.E., 651-2476. Popular
song writer Johnny Mercer was born in Savannah, Georgia, in 1909. Catchy tunes from
"Jeepers Creepers" (1938) and "That Old Black
Magic" (1942) to Oscar Award winners "Moon
River" (1961) and "Days of Wine and Roses"
(1962) are only a few of the songs for which Mercer will be remembered. In 1981, five years after
Mercer's death, his widow donated an extensive
collection of manuscripts, correspondence, photographs and awards to Georgia State University.
Hours: 8:30 a.m.-5 p.m. Monday-Friday.

㊸ Marietta/Cobb Museum of Art. 30
Atlanta St. N.E., Marietta, 424-8142. This fledg-
ling museum offers changing shows of historical
and contemporary artists. Hours: 11 a.m.-5 p.m.
Tuesday-Saturday.

**㊹ Monetary Museum/Federal Reserve
Bank.** 104 Marietta St. N.W., 521-8500. For anyone interested in the evolution of money, the history of banking in America, or fine examples of
rare coins, a trip to the Monetary Museum should
be on the agenda. Among the items which attract
the most attention are the rare 1792 "half-dime"
and a 1794 silver dollar (of which fewer than 100
exist today). Self-guided tours from 9 a.m.-4 p.m.
Monday-Friday. Visitors must be 14 years of age
or older. Group tours available.

45 **Zachor Holocaust Center.** Jewish Community Center, Lower Level, 1745 Peachtree Rd. N.E. The permanent exhibit covers holocaust history through photographs and memorabilia of survivors. Free admission. Hours: 1-4 p.m. Sunday.

AFRICAN-AMERICAN HERITAGE

46 **Apex (African American Panoramic Experience).** The John Wesley Dobbs Building, 135 Courtland, 521-APEX. Through exhibits detailing culture and heritage, you can experience the history of African-Americans in the United States: learn about famous black Atlantans, visit a period drugstore, or climb aboard a vintage trolley. Part of Apex is devoted to a gallery of African art called Sanokofa!, presented within the context of African contemporary music and photography. Cost: $2 for adults; $1 for students and senior citizens; free for children under 6. Hours: 10 a.m.-5 p.m. Tuesday-Saturday (open until 6 p.m. on Wednesday); 1-5 p.m., Sunday.

47 **Ebenezer Baptist Church.** 407-13 Auburn Ave. N.E., 688-7263. This famous church was once pastored by Martin Luther King, Jr., and before that by his father and his grandfather. Founded at another location in 1886, the present Gothic Revival structure was completed in 1922. King's body lay in state in the church in 1968, and his mother was assassinated in the sanctuary in 1974. Hours: 9 a.m.-4 p.m. Monday-Friday.

48 **The Herndon Home.** 587 University Place N.W., 581-9813. Atlanta University Center is the site where slavery-born Alonzo Herndon's fabulous home stands today. Although he began his career as a barber, Herndon went on to become Atlanta's wealthiest black with the establishment of the lucrative Atlanta Life Insurance Company. His 1910 15-room mansion in the Beaux Arts style was built by black craftsmen. After Herndon's death, his son Norris, who continued to run the insurance business, lived in the house until 1977. Since then, the house has been operated under the auspices of the Herndon Foundation. On display are original family furnishings and photos of black Atlantans from the 1800s to 1970s. The Venetian and Roman glass pieces (some of which are from 200 B.C.) were collected by Herndon's son and are particularly noteworthy. Silver and other decorative arts are exhibited, too. Hours: 10 a.m.-4 p.m. Tuesday-Saturday.

49 Martin Luther King, Jr., Boyhood Home. 501 Auburn Ave. N.E. This two-story structure in the Queen Anne style was built in 1895. Martin Luther King, Jr., was born in the house in 1929. The tour features photographs, original furnishings, and memorabilia of the King family. Hours: 10 a.m.-3:30 p.m. daily, September through May; 10 a.m.-5 p.m. daily, June through August. Hours are extended during the King Week celebration in January. Call 331-3919 for additional information.

50 Martin Luther King, Jr., Center For Nonviolent Social Change. 449 Auburn Ave. N.E. 524-1956. The King Center was established in 1968 "to preserve and advance Dr. King's unfinished work through teaching, interpreting, advocating and promoting nonviolently the elimination of poverty, racism, violence and war in quest of Dr. King's Beloved Community." The King Center, which boasts more than one million visitors per year, stands on a 44-acre site in the midst of a National Historic District. In the Freedom Hall Complex the visitor will encounter the Gandhi Room with its artifacts and memorabilia of Gandhi, the Rosa Parks Room honoring the mother of the Civil Rights Movement, a cafeteria, and a bookstore. In the Administration, Program and Archives Building, exhibition halls detail Dr. King's life and provide a continuous showing of films on his contributions to the struggle for civil rights in America. Here, too, are the King Library and Archives, which contain the world's largest collection of primary resource materials on the Civil Rights Movement and the most comprehensive collection of Dr. King's personal papers. Freedom Walkway, an outdoor colonnade, extends along the Reflecting Pool and leads to the Chapel of All Faiths. The tomb of Martin Luther King, Jr., is located here. On the face of the crypt are engraved the famous words of the leader: "Free at Last, Free at Last, Thank God Almighty I'm Free at Last." Hours: 9 a.m.-5:30 p.m. daily.

51 Martin Luther King, Jr., National Historic Site. 526 Auburn Ave. N.E., 331-3920. The birthplace of Martin Luther King, Jr., Ebenezer Baptist Church, and the grave of the civil rights leader are included in this 23.5-acre National Historic Site which is operated by the Department of the Interior. Tours of the site and the adjoining Sweet Auburn Preservation District are available at no charge upon request, Monday-Friday. Call for additional information.

52 Sweet Auburn. Auburn Area Revitalization Committee/Auburn Area Main Street Project offices are located at 250 Auburn Ave. N.E., 524-6754. Property along Auburn Ave., originally called Wheat Street, was purchased by former slaves after the Civil War. When the area began attracting prosperous black businesses, it was dubbed "Sweet Auburn Avenue" by John Wesley Dobbs, grandfather of Atlanta's current mayor, Maynard Jackson. Auburn Avenue was once referred to by *Forbes* as "the richest Negro street in America." Sweet Auburn is presently the subject of a revitalization plan aiming to restore the area to its former grandeur. Most of the buildings date from the late 1800s and early 1900s. In addition to the buildings which comprise the Martin Luther King, Jr., National Historic Site, other structures of note are the Odd Fellows Building at 228-50 Auburn Ave., Big Bethel African Methodist Episcopal Church with its landmark steeple bearing the large "Jesus Saves" sign, the Butler Street YMCA, which is significant for its political influence in the community, and the Rucker building, Atlanta's first black office building. Some of Atlanta's most prominent black businessmen chose Sweet Auburn as their business address, and the locale inspired many "firsts." The *Atlanta Daily World*, the nation's first black newspaper, was founded here, as was the first

black-owned radio station in America (WERD).
Both businesses continue to flourish at Sweet
Auburn locations today. Two extremely successful
black life insurance companies had their origins
on Sweet Auburn: Atlanta Life Insurance Co. and
Citizens Trust. Black nightclubs found their place
here, too. When Martin Luther King was a young
man, soul and blues legends such as Sam Cooke
and Otis Redding performed at the Royal Peacock
Lounge (still functioning as a nightclub, see
NIGHTLIFE, Blues). Sweet Auburn was a
street where the dreams of black men were real-
ized like no place else in the city.

FAMILY AND CHILDREN'S ACTIVITIES

53 American Adventures. On North Cobb Parkway in Marietta. Take I-75 North of Atlanta to Exit #113; exit on North Cobb Parkway and follow the signs, 424-WAVE. Adjacent to the popular White Water, American Adventures is an amusement park designed especially for small children. The park is open year round, so there are activities and rides both indoors and outdoors. Toddlers will love the Timber Line Truckers (convoy) and preschoolers will delight in the Ridgeline Racer roller coaster led by a fierce buffalo. Older children aren't completely left out either. There are two miniature golf courses requiring increasing levels of skill, bumper cars, and a Formula K car racetrack for the not-so-small. Free parking. Tickets may be purchased for individual rides or in booklet form. The best value is a combination White Water/American Adventures ticket if you have time to take in both attractions. Open daily except Christmas, but hours vary. Call for schedule.

54 Center for Puppetry Arts. 1404 Spring St. at 18th St. N.E., 874-0398 for information; box office: 873-3391. Founded in 1978 by the current executive director Vincent Anthony, the ribbon-cutting ceremony was attended by Kermit the Frog and his creator Jim Henson. The Muppets thus helped to launch this one-of-a-kind institution in the U.S. The newly renovated building con-

tains four theatres, a museum featuring permanent and traveling displays of puppets, a gift shop,
reference library, and educational facilities. Each
year the Center for Puppetry Arts produces a
family series adapted from classic stories, as well
as an adult series of shows. The elaborate productions definitely broaden the novice's idea of puppetry. Cost: $4.25 for performances; museum: $3
for ages 14 and older, but free with ticket to performance. Box office hours 9 a.m.-5 p.m. Monday-
Friday; 9 a.m.-4 p.m. Saturday. Museum hours: 9
a.m.-4 p.m. Monday-Saturday.

55 Fernbank Science Center. 156 Heaton
Park Dr. N.E., 378-4311. Owned and operated by
the DeKalb County School System, this children-
oriented science center focuses primarily on
astronomy and the natural sciences. The Exhibition Hall features taxidermy specimens revealing
animals in their natural environments and vanish-
ing habitats, especially focusing on species found
in Georgia from pre-history to the present. Kids
will love the dinosaur exhibit and the authentic
Apollo spacecraft. The Planetarium, one of the
world's largest, seats 500 under its 70-foot diame-
ter projection dome. Fernbank's Observatory,
with its huge 36-inch reflecting telescope, has
been instrumental in national research, live TV
broadcasts of Halley's Comet, and tracking of the
Apollo Lunar Missions. Fernbank's 18,000-volume
library makes it one of the leading science reference libraries in the Southeast. Cost for planetarium: $2 for adults; $1 for students; free for
senior citizens 62 and older. Hours: 8:30 a.m.-5
p.m. Monday; 8:30 a.m.-10 p.m. Tuesday-Friday;
10 a.m.-6 p.m. Saturday; and 1-5 p.m. Sunday.
The observatory is open to the public from dark
until 10 p.m. on **clear** Thursday and Friday
evenings.

56 Scitrek. 395 Piedmont Avenue, 522-5500.
Opened in 1988, this exciting hands-on science
and technology museum is the largest facility of
its kind in the Southeast. The museum is divided
into halls which represent different scientific
interests: in the Hall of Simple Machines, the visitor can lift a hundred-pound punching bag with

different levers and pulleys; in the Hall of Light and Perception, it is fun to create colored shadows; and in the Hall of Electricity and Magnetism, you can learn how electricity is produced by pedaling a bicycle; Kidspace is a wonderful entertainment and learning center for preschoolers. The Mathematics exhibit, sponsored by IBM, features the history and range of mathematics through a variety of demonstrations and visual displays. The gift store has all kinds of science-related toys, books and other items for sale. Cost: $6 for adults; $4 for children 3-17 and senior citizens 65 and older; special group rates are available. Hours: 10 a.m.-5 p.m. Tuesday-Saturday; noon-5 p.m. Sunday.

57 Six Flags Over Georgia. Located twelve miles west of Atlanta on I-20, 739-3400. This amusement park, featuring rides, arcade games, musical reviews and special entertainment, offers fun for the whole family. The Georgia Cyclone, a wooden roller coaster patterned after the legendary Coney Island Cyclone, is a heart-stopper for the most intrepid thrill-seeker. Special extravaganzas are planned for Halloween, the Christmas holidays, and New Year's Eve. Cost: $20.95 for adults; $14.95 for children 3-9; $10.38 for senior citizens 55 and older; free for children under 3. Opens at 10 a.m.; closing time varies. Open daily from Memorial Day through Labor Day.

58 "Spectacles." High Museum of Art, 1280 Peachtree St. N.E. in the Woodruff Arts Center, 898-9535. Located in the Junior Gallery on the bottom level of the High Museum, this participatory exhibit is designed to acquaint children with lines, color, perspective, and texture. Activities such as the illuminated shape board and a large Velcro wall provide interesting stimulus for hands and minds. Cost: (included in museum admission price) $4 for adults; $1 for children 6-17; free for children under 6. (On Thursday the museum is open free to the public from 1-5 p.m.) Hours: 2-4:30 p.m. Tuesday-Friday; 10 a.m.-4:30 p.m. Saturday; noon-4:30 p.m. Sunday. Closed Monday.

59 Stone Mountain Memorial Park. Located 16 miles east of Atlanta on Hwy. 78, 498-5702. Around the world's largest outcropping of exposed granite sprawls this 3200-acre park with multi-recreational and family activities. The mountain itself is distinguished by a monumental carving which took over 50 years to complete and measures 90 x 190 feet, making it the world's largest high-relief sculpture. The carving shows Confederate President Jefferson Davis and Generals Robert E. Lee and "Stonewall" Jackson on horseback. Among the many activities the visitor can choose from are a tour around the mountain on the Scenic Railroad; a trip to the top of the mountain via the Skylift cable car or on foot along a nature trail; a relaxing cruise on the lake aboard the paddlewheel riverboat; an exploration of Civil War artifacts on exhibit at Memorial Hall, and a look at an authentic antebellum plantation. Other attractions include the Antique Auto and Music Museum, the Wildlife Trails featuring animals once indigenous to Georgia, and a special petting farm small children will enjoy. The Laser Show on the north face of the mountain is a popular evening diversion during the late spring through early fall. The multitude of recreational possibilities include ice skating, tennis, hiking, biking, mini-golf, batting in cages, golf, boating and fishing, swimming, and a gigantic playground for the children with a multi-level play structure. Stone Mountain will serve as the venue for the water sports in the 1996 Summer Olympics to be held in Atlanta. The park contains two hotel complexes: the Stone Mountain Inn (469-3311) and the 250-room Evergreen Conference Center and Resort (879-9900). All kinds of eating facilities are available throughout the park. Cost: one-day park permit per car is $5; annual permit is $20; major attraction prices are $2.50 for adults and $1.50 for children 3-11, unless otherwise noted. Hours: park gates are open from 6 a.m. to midnight daily. Major attractions open at 10 a.m. and close anywhere from 7-8:30 p.m. in the summer, but around 5 p.m. other seasons.

60 White Water. On North Cobb Parkway in Marietta. Take I-75 North of Atlanta to Exit #113; exit on North Cobb Parkway and follow the signs, 424-WAVE. Fun for the family abounds in this 35-acre water park, with flumes and raft rides, a wave pool, a tidal wave, and a special area for the little ones called Little Squirt's Island. Restaurants, a gift shop, and shower and locker facilities are available. White Water is next door to American Adventures, a theme park for young children; combination tickets can be purchased for the two attractions at a discount. Cost: $14.99 for adults and children taller than 48"; $9.99 for children age 4 up to 48" in height; free for children under 4 and senior citizens 62 and older. Open 10 a.m. daily from Memorial Day to Labor Day; open weekends in May.

61 Yellow River Game Ranch. 4525 Highway 78, Lilburn, 972-6643. Take a one-mile nature hike through a 24-acre game preserve and you'll observe more than 600 animals. You are encouraged to feed and touch the domestic animals and deer. Children will love interacting with the rabbits in the bunny burrows, and they'll remember the herd of buffalo and the mountain lions, too. Picnic tables are located throughout the park and there is a gift shop at the entrance. Cost: $3.50 for adults; $2.50 for children 3-11; one child under 3 admitted free with a paying adult; group prices available. Hours: 9:30 a.m.-6 p.m. daily; 9:30 a.m.-dusk in the summer.

62 Zoo Atlanta. 800 Cherokee Ave. S.E., 624-5650. Although over a century old, the zoo is making a comeback in a big way. In an attempt to become one of the premier zoos in the world, Zoo Atlanta has been undergoing a multi-million-dollar redevelopment program for several years. Animals can now be viewed in environments simulating their natural habitats, and visitors are treated to educational demonstrations and programs which stress conservation and the importance of protecting endangered species. The Ford African Rain Forest is home to gorillas from the Yerkes Regional Primate Research Center of Emory

University, as well as to Willie B., the gorilla who is the zoo's most famous inhabitant. The endangered black rhino shares the tall grasses with giraffes, ostriches, and antelopes in the Masai Mara complex which replicates the plains of East Africa. New exhibits are opening continuously, but already there is much to see. Small children will enjoy the petting zoo and train ride. Eating facilities and a gift shop are also located on the premises. Cost: $6.75 for adults; $4 for children 3-11; free for children 2 and younger; $5.75 for senior citizens ages 60 and older, Monday-Friday. Group rates available. Hours: 10 a.m.-4:30 p.m. daily. During daylight saving time, closing is extended by one hour on weekends. Closed major holidays.

MAJOR COLLEGES AND UNIVERSITIES

63 Agnes Scott College. Founded in 1889 as The Decatur Female Seminary, the liberal arts college is still primarily a women's school and is located east of Atlanta in Decatur. The grounds are characterized by majestic red-brick buildings, ancient oaks, and shady magnolias.

64 Atlanta University Complex. Seven black colleges comprise this complex in southwest Atlanta. Morehouse College, an-all male school; Spelman College, an all-female school; Morris Brown; and Clark College are the undergraduate schools. The schools with graduate programs are Atlanta University, the Interdenominational Theological Center, and the Morehouse School of Medicine.

65 Emory University. Founded in Oxford, Georgia, in 1838, the main campus was moved to an intown neighborhood in Atlanta in 1919. The old part of the campus is most picturesque with its pink-and-grey marble buildings, crowned by red-tile roofs, positioned on grassy quadrangles. The university is recognized as a center of progressive thinking in the South.

66 Georgia Institute of Technology.
Chartered by the state General Assembly in 1885, the school opened its doors three years later as the Georgia School of Technology. Located west of I-75 in downtown Atlanta, the university is highly acclaimed in the fields of engineering and the sciences.

67 Georgia State University.
This downtown university near the State Capitol has an enrollment which rivals that of the University of Georgia (an hour away in Athens). The school emphasizes graduate programs and offers no boarding facilities, so the student population is generally older than at most campuses.

68 Kennesaw State College.
Founded in 1963 as a junior college, the school gained four-year status in 1979. Currently, this liberal arts college north of Atlanta in Kennesaw boasts 10,000 students and an expanding graduate program.

69 Mercer University.
Affiliated with the Southern Baptist Convention, Mercer's main campus lies in Macon. The Atlanta campus, founded in 1972 after the merger of Mercer University and Atlanta Baptist College, is located in northeast Atlanta.

70 Oglethorpe University.
Named after General James Oglethorpe, founder of the state of Georgia, the small liberal arts college, chartered in 1835, began construction on its campus in northeast Atlanta in 1915. Gothic architecture distinguishes the campus which is now the home of the Georgia Shakespeare Festival.

UNDERGROUND

In the 1840s what now comprises downtown
Atlanta was the end of the railroad line. Ware-
houses and shops lined streets that ran near the
railroad. In time, viaducts were constructed over
the streets for streetcars, and eventually these
byways were paved over. The stores and ware-
houses left beneath the roads were abandoned or
turned into basement storage for structures front-
ing on the streets above, and they remained
unused and forgotten until the 1960s.

Underground Atlanta first opened as a tourist
attraction in the late 1960s, but its popularity
gradually waned, and many of the existing buildings were destroyed by vandals and fire. However,
with typical Atlanta spirit, the city decided to res-
urrect this once-teeming entertainment center,
and the new Underground was born in the summer of 1989. In the Underground of today, visitors
will discover a blend of the old and the new. Many
authentic storefronts and historic buildings have
been restored, while the main entry to Underground at Peachtree Fountains Plaza is testimony
to more contemporary cityscaping. Here the visitor is greeted by Underground's new landmark, a
soaring ten-story light tower and cascading fountains. This courtyard connects with Upper Alabama Street, home to many smart fashion shops.
Lower Alabama and Lower Pryor streets (the
original streets of old Atlanta and the site of old
Underground) can be reached via stairs or escala-
tor. Packinghouse Row, where many of Atlanta's
first meat packers and food wholesalers thrived,

now showcases a variety of eateries and foodstuff operations. Kenny's Alley is a three-story entertainment complex which boasts some of the city's most exciting night spots. A lot of fun is packed into Underground's twelve acres, fun for every member of the family.

In addition to the entertainment and eating establishments, Underground offers a number of attractive retail establishments. Shoppers will be familiar with some of the national chain stores like Eddie Bauer, Victoria's Secret and Ann Taylor. Of the many smaller franchises or locally-owned businesses, a representative sample is provided here. Pushcarts create a street-market effect along Lower Alabama St., their vendors hawking everything from soft goods to jewelry and objets d'art.

Underground is located between Peachtree St. and Central Ave. at Alabama St., 523-2311. Adequate parking is available nearby, but Underground is readily accessible by the MARTA train from the Five Points Station or from the MARTA Peachtree Trolley. Hours: 10 a.m.-9:30 p.m. Monday-Saturday; Noon-6 p.m. Sunday. Restaurant and club hours vary.

HISTORICAL SITES AND POINTS OF INTEREST

1 Atlanta Heritage Row. Upper Alabama St. between Pryor St. and Central Ave., 584-7879. Follow the timeline corridor from Atlanta's beginnings in the Georgia wilderness to its present status as a cosmopolitan city. The history exhibits highlight Atlanta's past with the use of audio and visual technology. You can hear the din of the trains in 1850, listen to the rousing voice of Henry Grady in his New South speech of 1886, see a newsreel of F.D.R. opening the subsidized housing development of Techwood Homes in 1940, and watch the latest news from CNN. Another exhibit envisions Atlanta's role in the future. Cost: $4 for adults; $3 for students, seniors, and tours; $2 for children 3-12. Hours: 10 a.m.-7 p.m., Tuesday-Saturday; 1-7 p.m., Sunday. Closed on Monday.

2 The New Georgia Railroad. 1 Martin Luther King, Jr., Dr. S.W., 656-0769. Enjoy a ride on the 18-mile Atlanta Loop or choose the Stone Mountain Village and Park Ride in a restored railcar. The railroad has three engines — two steam engines built in 1910 and 1911, and a streamlined diesel that used to pull the Southern Crescent. The train journey begins at the Zero Mile Marker — a stone designating where the city of Atlanta (originally known as Terminus, and later Marthasville) began at a railroad crossway. Cost: $10 for adults and $5 for children on the

Atlanta Loop. $12.50 for adults and $5 for children on the Stone Mountain Village and Park route. Hours: Train departs at 10 a.m., noon, and 2 p.m. on Saturday. A Dinner Train runs Thursday-Saturday nights for $39.50 per person. Reservations must be made by the Monday prior to departure.

❸ The World of Coca-Cola. 55 Martin Luther King, Jr., Dr. (at Central Ave.), across from Kenny's Alley entrance to Underground Atlanta, 676-5151. At the entrance to this modern pavilion hangs a giant neon Coca-Cola sign, a familiar sight to Americans and international visitors alike. This museum records the history of the drink that made Atlanta famous. Suspended from the skylit atrium are flags from the 160 countries where Coke is distributed. It is a high-tech gallery with many interactive exhibits that the young will love, but it contains lots of nostalgia and memorabilia to please the older crowd, too. Visitors will see an amazing bottling demonstration, be treated to a presentation by a talented "soda jerk" in a model of a 1930s soda fountain, and tour the world of Coke through audio, video and photographic exhibits. An amazing high-tech soda fountain will wow you with neon lights, sound effects, and geysers of the bubbly stuff spewing forth from transparent columns. You can also sample other Coca-Cola products from around the world, some acrid, and others sickeningly sweet. The Trade Mart on the lower level is a shop devoted to Coca-Cola-related merchandise, from shirts and toys to Christmas ornaments and radios. Cost: $2.50, adults; $2, seniors; $1.50, children 6-12; free for children under 6. Hours: 10 a.m.-9:30 p.m., Monday-Saturday; noon-6 p.m., Sunday. Closed on major holidays. Reservations are suggested: call 676-5151 from 9 a.m.-5 p.m., Monday-Friday.

RESTAURANTS

4 Buck's. Lower Alabama at Lower Pryor St. or Upper Alabama at Upper Pryor St., 525-2825. Standing two-stories tall, Buck's fronts on Peachtree Fountains Plaza and can also be entered from lower Alabama St. Part of the Atlanta-based chain of Peasant restaurants, Buck's specializes in burgers and dogs, chicken grills, pasta, and salad. Antique furnishings soften the austerity of the black, red, and white decor. Hours: 11 a.m.-1 a.m., Monday-Thursday; 11 a.m.-11 p.m., Friday and Saturday; noon-10:30 p.m., Sunday. Major credit cards. Casual. Moderate prices.

5 Caribbean Sunset. Kenny's Alley, ground floor, 659-4589. Entering this establishment flanked by aquariums with exotic fish, you find the sounds and flavors of island life seductive. Among the many tempting entrees, you can enjoy Jamaican jerk chicken and stuffed red-eye snapper to the sounds of reggae and calypso music. Hours: 4 p.m.-midnight, Monday-Thursday; 4 p.m.-3 a.m., Friday; 2 p.m.-3 a.m., Saturday; 4 p.m.-midnight, Sunday. Music from 9 p.m.-midnight, Sunday-Thursday; 9 p.m.-1 a.m., Friday and Saturday. Major credit cards. Casual. Moderate prices. Cover charge is $5 on Friday and Saturday, but no charge during the rest of the week.

⑥ Fat Tuesday. Kenny's Alley, ground floor, 523-7404. A popular watering hole specializing in frozen daiquiris and New Orleans-style, short-order foods. With twenty drink machines, their frozen concoctions range from the simple straw-berry daiquiri to the explosive "swamp water" which combines six fruit juices with five liquors. Open 11 a.m.-12:30 a.m., Monday-Thursday; 11 a.m.-1:30 a.m., Friday and Saturday; 12:30 p.m.-12:30 a.m., Sunday. Major credit cards. Casual. Moderate prices.

⑦ J.W. Pilgreen's Original Bar & Grill. Kenny's Alley, third level, 522-6917. An Atlanta establishment since 1932, this eatery is well known for its steaks, barbecued ribs, and chicken. The lounge features local acts which range from '50s music to jazz. Open 11 a.m.-11 p.m., Monday-Saturday for lunch and dinner; opens at noon on Sunday. The lounge is open until 2 a.m., nightly, with music beginning at 8 p.m. Major credit cards. Reservations accepted. Casual. Moderate prices.

⑧ Lombardi's. Upper Pryor St. or Kenny's Alley, third level, 522-6568. See **RESTAU-RANTS, Downtown.**

⑨ Old Alabama Eatery Food Court. Fast food heaven with choices galore. Sample a gyro at **The Middle East Connection** or fried chicken from **Southern Vittles**. If you are watching your waistline, you can select a salad from **The Cafe Manet** or savor a bowl of soup from **Schlotzsky's**. Indulge in a fruit smoothie at **Udderly Cool** or treat yourself to homemade ice cream at **Gorin's Ice Cream**. Each family member can choose a different gourmet and eth-nic fare and convene at a table in the court for a quick, tasty, and inexpensive meal.

⑩ Ruby Red's Southern Pavilion. 76 Wall St. (corner of Wall and Pryor Sts.), 577-4800. New home to the Ruby Red's of old Underground. The fondly-remembered, good-time bar has burgeoned in size. The Ruby Red Room is modeled after the original Ruby Red's with its peanut-shell floor, and it rings with banjo tunes. Yet it occupies only a portion of this 12,000 square foot space. In the Sunday Room you can sample a dinner of New South cuisine. You can stop in for a brew at O'Hara's Bar or just browse through the souvenir shop. Banquet facilities are also available. Hours: 11 a.m.-2 a.m., daily. Music runs from 9 a.m.-1 a.m., nightly. Major credit cards. Casual.

⓫ **Tortilla Flats.** Kenny's Alley, ground floor or Lower Pryor, 522-0844. Relax and fill up on Tex-Mex food at this Mexican cantina. Sizzling fajitas are a tempting treat. You can dine inside or on the patio that overlooks the mall. Open 11 a.m.-11 p.m., Monday-Thursday; 11 a.m.-midnight, Friday and Saturday; and noon-10 p.m., Sunday. Major credit cards. Casual. Moderate prices.

NIGHTLIFE

⓬ **The A-Train.** Kenny's Alley, ground floor, 221-0522. Experience the electrical atmosphere in this nightclub featuring contemporary and progressive jazz, showcasing both local and national talent. Open 5 p.m.-12:30 a.m., Monday-Thursday; 5 p.m.-2:30 a.m., Friday and Saturday; noon-3 p.m. for Sunday brunch and 6 p.m.-1 a.m. for Sunday evening entertainment. Music starts between 8 and 8:30 p.m., daily. Mixed drinks. Major credit cards. Reservations accepted. Cosmopolitan attire. Serves food. Cover charge varies according to act.

⓭ **Atlanta's Beach Club.** Kenny's Alley, ground floor, 577-9283. Dance to '60s and '70s beach music and hit tunes through the present. A boardwalk surrounding a sand pit is illuminated by palm trees with neon leaves. Opens nightly at 7 p.m. The deejay starts spinning records at 9 p.m. Mixed drinks. Major credit cards. Casual. Average cover charge is $3, but may vary on occasion.

⑭ Banks & Shane. Lower Pryor St., 577-4300. After an eighteen-year tenure in Atlanta, Banks & Shane have built a large and loyal following. They perform Wednesday-Saturday nights at their club. In addition to their act, they bring a variety of music to their dinner-theatre-type club, ranging from folk and pop to bluegrass and big band. Open 11 a.m.-midnight, Monday-Saturday; closed Sunday. Mixed drinks. Major credit cards. Casual. Serves food. No cover Monday and Tuesday; $5 cover charge Wednesday-Saturday. Cover varies on special acts. Reservations suggested.

⑮ Blues Harbor. Kenny's Alley, ground floor, 524-3001. The sounds of Chicago-style and Delta blues can accompany a Maine lobster dinner while you experience the magic of the bluenote. Opens daily at 6 p.m. Music starts at 9:30 p.m. Serves food. Mixed drinks. Casual. Cover charge varies with act.

⑯ Dante's Down the Hatch. Lower Pryor St., 577-1800. Dante's is the only club to return to its original location in Underground. The building itself has a fascinating history beginning in 1850 as The Planter's Hotel. At Dante's you may dine on a replica of an eighteenth-century sailing frigate surrounded by a moat where live crocodiles swim. The boat is anchored to a wharf where you may opt for a different kind of music with dinner. Open 3 p.m.-midnight, Monday-Thursday; 3 p.m.-1 a.m., Friday; 2 p.m.-1 a.m., Saturday; 2-11 p.m, Sunday. The Brothers Three Trio plays jazz on the ship starting at 8 p.m., Monday-Saturday. On Sunday you can hear the Little Big Band play jazz beginning at 7 p.m. Folk or acoustical guitar is featured on the wharf daily, beginning at 5 p.m. Mixed drinks. Major credit cards. Reservations encouraged. Serves food. Cover charge added to check is $5 for the ship and $1 for the wharf.

🔟 Groundhog Tavern. Kenny's Alley, ground floor, 659-2296. A friendly spot with a neighborhood-bar-and-grill feel. Burgers, soups, salads, and pasta are popular lunch fare and steaks are an evening specialty. Eat indoors or enjoy the open-air patio in Kenny's Alley. Open 11:15 a.m.-3 a.m., Monday-Saturday; 12:30 p.m.-2 a.m., Sunday. Mixed drinks. Major credit cards. Casual. No cover charge.

🔟 Lilly's Pub. Kenny's Alley, ground floor, 524-5459. In the midst of the crowded tourist tunnels of Underground, it's pleasant to retreat to this oasis with its neighborhood-bar ambience. Sub sandwiches are sold by the inch. The pasta bar and entertainment attract folks to the week-day Happy Hour from 5-8 p.m. Opens at 11:30 a.m., daily. A piano player entertains with music ranging from ballads to Elton John and Billy Joel, from 9 p.m.-1 a.m., Wednesday-Saturday. Mixed drinks. Major credit cards. Casual. Serves food. No cover charge.

🔟 LTL Ditty's. 94 Pryor St. S.W., second level, 522-2977. Enjoy the live entertainment sounds of '50s and '60s rock 'n roll (all the oldies you've been wanting to hear) at LTL Ditty's. Music from 7:30 p.m.-1:30 a.m., Monday-Thursday; 7:30 p.m.-2:30 a.m., Friday and Saturday. Mixed drinks. Major credit cards. Casual. Snack food only. Cover charge: $4, Friday and Saturday nights only.

🔟 Miss Kitty's Saloon and Dance Hall. Kenny's Alley, ground floor, 524-4614. Dance to the sounds of country & western and southern rock in this late 1800s authentic-style saloon. Bar-becue is the featured fare. Open 11 a.m.-2 a.m., Sunday-Thursday; 11 a.m.-4 a.m., Friday; 11 a.m.-3 a.m., Saturday. Music starts at 8:30 p.m., Sunday-Thursday; 9 p.m., Friday and Saturday. Mixed drinks. Major credit cards. Casual. Cover charge: $2, Sunday-Thursday; $4, Friday and Saturday.

㉑ The Punch Line, Underground. Kenny's Alley, ground floor, 681-5337. Continuing to uphold The Punch Line's reputation as a national comedy club, the Underground location has added music to its daily schedule of events. Opens nightly at 7 p.m. The comedy show starts at 8:30 p.m. and live music and dancing begin at 10 p.m. Mixed drinks. Major credit cards. Serves food. Cover charge varies by act and day. Call for reservations and prices.

㉒ T-Bird's. Upper Alabama St., 525-0881. Bop and twist your way around the dance floor to the sounds of '50s and '60s music. Nostalgic decor for older baby boomers and up. Occasional live acts. Serves food. Mixed drinks. Major credit cards. Casual. Another location in Stone Mountain.

SHOPPING

㉓ Antiquities Historical Galleries. Lower Alabama St., 525-1591. A plethora of prints, maps, paintings, autographs, and Civil War memorabilia are for sale in this museum-like gallery. A fun place to browse even if you can't afford some of the high-ticket items. Hours: 10 a.m.-9:30 p.m., Monday-Saturday and noon-6 p.m., Sunday.

㉔ Barnie's Coffee and Tea Company. Lower Alabama St., Packinghouse Row, 577-1703. In addition to their array of coffees and teas, Barnie's carries a large selection of mugs, espresso cups, and teapots. Gift baskets are a popular item. Hours: 10 a.m.-10 p.m., Monday-Thursday; 10 a.m.-11 p.m., Friday and Saturday; noon-6 p.m., Sunday.

㉕ Effie's. Lower Alabama St., 659-1391. Victoriana is the predominant theme of this boutique specializing in women's vintage clothing. In addition to the apparel, a complementary assortment of gifts and jewelry are for sale. Hours: 10 a.m.-9:30 p.m., Monday-Saturday; noon-6 p.m., Sunday. Also a location at Lenox Square.

㉖ Georgia Grand Central. Corner of Lower Alabama St. and Lower Pryor St., 577-3335. Plunge into the past as you savor the flavor and aromas of a turn-of-the-century general store. Here you can find everything from old-fashioned hard candy and regional food items to nostalgia giftware and antique replicas. Hours: 10 a.m.-9:30 p.m., Monday-Saturday; noon-6 p.m., Sunday.

27 Georgiou. Lower Alabama St., 523-5552. A single-designer store specializing in women's clothing made from natural fibers, especially raw silk. Garments are designed to be interchangeable. Accessories, shoes, and jewelry can be coordinated with your selections, too. Hours: 10 a.m.-9:30 p.m., Monday-Saturday; noon-6 p.m., Sunday.

28 The Gifted Hand. Upper Alabama St., 659-6810. Hand-blown glass, metal and ceramic sculpture, American crafts, fine-art jewelry, stained-glass pieces, and contemporary art of all sorts are for sale in this gallery on the upper level. Hours: 10 a.m.-9:30 p.m., Monday-Saturday; noon-6 p.m. Sunday. The Gifted Hand has another metro location in Roswell.

29 Hattitudes. Old Alabama St., 681-0086. All types of men's and women's hats, from berets and tams to fedoras and sombreros. Men's and women's accessories, as well as designer hats, are part of their inventory. Hours: 10 a.m.-10 p.m., Monday-Saturday; noon-6 p.m., Sunday.

30 Koala Blue. Lower Alabama St., 658-9773. Australian-inspired sportswear for fashion-forward women. One of Olivia Newton John's chain of stores. Hours: 10 a.m.-9:30 p.m., Monday-Saturday; noon-6 p.m., Sunday. Also located at Perimeter Mall.

31 Logo Depot. Old Alabama St., 221-0805. Sweats and T's, glassware and mugs emblazoned with the Underground logo. Atlanta 1996 Olympics wear, too. Hours: 10 a.m.-10 p.m., Monday-Saturday; noon-6 p.m., Sunday.

32 Papier D'Couleur. Upper Alabama St., Packinghouse Row, 577-7854. A wide variety of Latin American papier-mache gift items. Lots of parrots, flamingos, vegetables, and masks. A festive, market atmosphere. Hours: 10 a.m.-9:30 p.m., Monday-Saturday; noon-6 p.m., Sunday.

㉝ S.O.T.A. Lower Alabama St., 524-8829. European-designed men's clothing in rayon and silk. Casual and fun styles with a contemporary flare. From shirts and pants to shoes and accessories, S.O.T.A. can outfit the male from head to toe. Hours: 10 a.m.-9:30 p.m., Monday-Saturday; noon-6 p.m., Sunday.

㉞ Sox Appeal. Upper Alabama St., 577-1500. Men's, women's, and children's socks and stockings, from the conservative to the wild. Hours: 10 a.m.-10 p.m., Monday-Thursday; 10 a.m.-midnight, Friday and Saturday; noon-6 p.m., Sunday.

㉟ Tannery West. Upper Alabama St., 681-1673. Fashionable leather clothing for men and women is the specialty of Tannery West. Trendy skirts, pants, jackets, and shirts are constructed from high-quality lambskin. Hours: 10 a.m.-9:30 p.m., Monday-Saturday; noon-6 p.m., Sunday.

㊱ Tie Rack of London. Upper Alabama St., 577-1840. A huge selection of men's ties, bow ties, and cummerbunds all the way from the ultra-conservative to the cutting edge. Braces, handkerchiefs, and ladies' Italian wool scarves and wraps are also alluring. Hours: 10 a.m.-9:30 p.m., Monday-Saturday; noon-6 p.m., Sunday.

㊲ The Verandah. Upper Alabama St., 659-1549. Unique gifts from around the world, including Victorian ornaments and teapots, collectible porcelain dolls, and *Gone With The Wind* memorabilia. Hours: 10 a.m.-9:30 p.m., Monday-Saturday; noon-6 p.m., Sunday.

THE ARTS

Atlanta attracts visitors from throughout the Southeast who are hungry for a taste of live drama, professional dance, or classical music, or who wish to broaden their knowledge of fine art or add to their individual collections. Although the state of the arts in the city is frequently on rocky financial footing, the spirit of the art community breathes with life. The status of the performing and visual arts has become more cosmopolitan within the last few years, fortifying Atlanta's image as an international city.

Theatre listings selected for inclusion are by no means complete, but are intended to reflect the variety and quality of theatre-going opportunities available in Atlanta. Art galleries are chosen and reviewed by Catherine Fox, Visual Art Critic for the *Atlanta Journal-Constitution*. As for the many and varied dance troupes in the city, from the Atlanta Ballet to jazz dance companies, schedules and locations of performances may be ascertained through the local media. The Atlanta Symphony Orchestra, under the direction of Yoel Levi, is highly recommended. Call 898-1182 to reach the box office or 876-HORN for recorded information concerning current programming of the symphony.

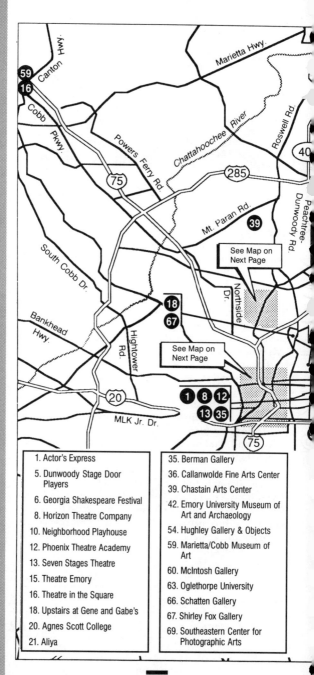

1. Actor's Express
5. Dunwoody Stage Door Players
6. Georgia Shakespeare Festival
8. Horizon Theatre Company
10. Neighborhood Playhouse
12. Phoenix Theatre Academy
13. Seven Stages Theatre
15. Theatre Emory
16. Theatre in the Square
18. Upstairs at Gene and Gabe's
20. Agnes Scott College
21. Aliya

35. Berman Gallery
36. Callanwolde Fine Arts Center
39. Chastain Arts Center
42. Emory University Museum of Art and Archaeology
54. Hughley Gallery & Objects
59. Marietta/Cobb Museum of Art
60. McIntosh Gallery
63. Oglethorpe University
66. Schatten Gallery
67. Shirley Fox Gallery
69. Southeastern Center for Photographic Arts

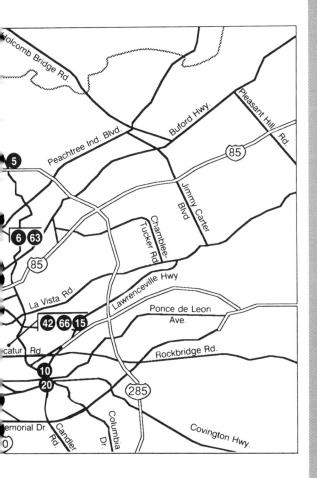

THE ARTS MAP

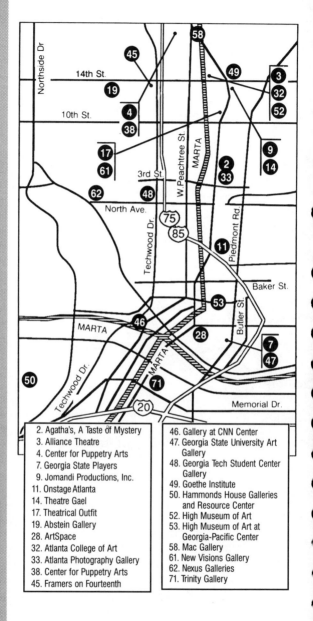

2. Agatha's, A Taste of Mystery
3. Alliance Theatre
4. Center for Puppetry Arts
7. Georgia State Players
9. Jomandi Productions, Inc.
11. Onstage Atlanta
14. Theatre Gael
17. Theatrical Outfit
19. Abstein Gallery
28. ArtSpace
32. Atlanta College of Art
33. Atlanta Photography Gallery
38. Center for Puppetry Arts
45. Framers on Fourteenth

46. Gallery at CNN Center
47. Georgia State University Art Gallery
48. Georgia Tech Student Center Gallery
49. Goethe Institute
50. Hammonds House Galleries and Resource Center
52. High Museum of Art
53. High Museum of Art at Georgia-Pacific Center
58. Mac Gallery
61. New Visions Gallery
62. Nexus Galleries
71. Trinity Gallery

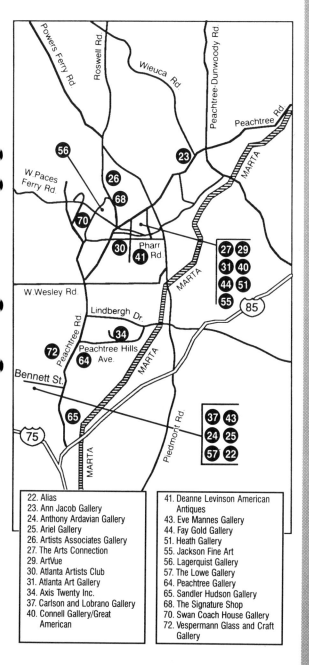

22. Alias
23. Ann Jacob Gallery
24. Anthony Ardavian Gallery
25. Ariel Gallery
26. Artists Associates Gallery
27. The Arts Connection
29. ArtVue
30. Atlanta Artists Club
31. Atlanta Art Gallery
34. Axis Twenty Inc.
37. Carlson and Lobrano Gallery
40. Connell Gallery/Great American

41. Deanne Levinson American Antiques
43. Eve Mannes Gallery
44. Fay Gold Gallery
51. Heath Gallery
55. Jackson Fine Art
56. Lagerquist Gallery
57. The Lowe Gallery
64. Peachtree Gallery
65. Sandler Hudson Gallery
68. The Signature Shop
70. Swan Coach House Gallery
72. Vespermann Glass and Craft Gallery

PERFORMING ARTS

In addition to the established theatres and community theatres listed here, Theatre of the Stars (252-8960) and Theatre League of Atlanta (873-4300) bring touring productions to Atlanta on an annual basis which represent the best of recent Broadway hits and revivals. Call for reservations and schedule of performances.

❶ Actor's Express. 280 Elizabeth St., 221-0831. The three-year-old Actor's Express, the "metro area's newest and hottest theatre company," according to the *Atlanta Journal-Constitution*, is located in historic Inman Park near Little Five Points. The goal of the theatre is to produce a consciously provocative mix of contemporary and classic plays. The work is socially relevant, innovative, and imaginative; the theatre is intimate and relaxed.

❷ Agatha's, A Taste of Mystery. 693 Peachtree St. N.E., 875-1610. In this unique dinner theatre, diners participate in solving a murder mystery over a five-course dinner with wine. The performances have a ten-week run and are all original productions. Hours: 7:30 p.m., Tuesday-Saturday; 7 p.m., Sunday. Available seven days a week for group reservations.

❸ Alliance Theatre. 1280 Peachtree St. N.E., 892-2414. Under the talented direction of Kenny Leon, this long-established Atlanta theatre features a season of musical, classical and

contemporary productions on its 750-seat mainstage. The Alliance Studio Theatre produces a
season ranging from premieres of new plays to
off-Broadway and regional hit productions. The
Alliance Children's Theatre performs several
times a year. The Alliance is part of the Atlanta
Arts Alliance and is housed in the Robert W.
Woodruff Arts Center.

4 Center for Puppetry Arts. See
**ATTRACTIONS. Family and Children's
Activities**.

5 Dunwoody Stage Door Players. 5339
Chamblee Dunwoody Rd., North Dekalb Cultural
Center, 396-1726. Call 458-7743 for reservations.
This little theatre company, organized in 1974,
has proven its popularity by its longevity. Now in
its first permanent home, current programming
includes a Mainstage series of five plays, a Second
Stage Series for the development of works in pro-
gress by local playwrights, and a summer New
Works Festival.

6 Georgia Shakespeare Festival.
Oglethorpe University, 4484 Peachtree Rd. N.E.,
264-0020. From its inception in 1984, this non-
profit company has dedicated itself to the presentation of high quality Shakespeare productions.
The first plays were staged in 1986, and since that
time the attendance at performances has quad-
rupled. The season runs from June through
August and productions are held in a large tent
on the campus. Picnicking is allowed on the Festival grounds prior to the performances.

7 Georgia State Players. Georgia State University, Alumni Hall, 30 Courtland St., 651-2225.
The oldest active theatre company in Atlanta produces five plays annually, including musicals,
drama and comedy among its selections. Actors
are drawn from the student and faculty population of Georgia State University as well as the
general public.

8 Horizon Theatre Company. 1038 Austin Ave. N.E. in Little Five Points, 584-7450. Founded in 1983, the Horizon Theatre Company premieres contemporary plays ranging from satire to drama. The mission of the Horizon Theatre has been to bring plays about our changing world to the public. Plays run October through May.

9 Jomandi Productions, Inc. Performances are held at the 14th St. Playhouse, 14th St. at Juniper in Midtown; box office: 892-0880; administrative offices: 876-6346. The word Jomandi means "people gathered for celebration." Jomandi has been heralding the African-American experience in drama since its inception in 1978. The company maintains a mainstage and a tour program. More than half of Jomandi's productions are original, and stage adaptations have been made from the literary works of such renowned black writers as Sonia Sanchez, Toni Cade Bambara, Maya Angelou, James Baldwin, Jean Toomer, and Langston Hughes. The company is led by co-artistic directors Marsha Jackson and Thomas W. Jones II, both of whom are actors and playwrights.

10 Neighborhood Playhouse. 430 West Trinity Place, Decatur, 373-5311. Neighborhood Playhouse was one of the first repertory theatres in the Atlanta-metro area to offer year-round performances. Since its inception in 1979, Neighborhood Playhouse has grown from a small theater to a major contributor to the arts in Atlanta. It is currently one of the few Atlanta theatres producing a One Act Festival. Neighborhood Playhouse is active in outreach programs and cooperative ventures in children's theatre, too.

11 Onstage Atlanta. 420 Courtland St. N.E., 897-1802. Formerly known as the DeKalb Little Theatre, the company moved downtown in 1973 and changed its name to Onstage Atlanta. In 1980 it moved into a converted car repair garage which provided a seating capacity of 140. Onstage

Atlanta remains Atlanta's longest running, most intimate theatre. A subscription season of five to six plays includes musicals, drama, and comedy.

12 Phoenix Theatre Academy. Performances are held at the Seven Stages Theatre, 1105 Euclid Ave., Little Five Points; box office: 523-7647 at Seven Stages; administrative offices: 365-8088. The demise of the Academy Theatre in 1989 was a severe blow to the Atlanta arts community, but the reformation of that theatre under the direction of the highly respected founder and artistic director, Frank Wittow, was a happy occasion for the city. Appropriately renamed the Phoenix Theatre Academy, the new company is built on the foundation of Georgia's oldest professional resident theatre company. A Theatre for Youth, A New Play program and a Human Service Program are all important components of the company's outreach programs. Barbara Lebow remains Playwright-in-Residence. The mainstage season is currently produced at the Seven Stages Theatre.

13 Seven Stages Theatre. 1105 Euclid Ave., Little Five Points; box office: 523-7647; administrative office: 522-0911. Located in the heart of the counter-culture district of Atlanta, this theatre company seeks to bring issue-oriented themes to the stage. Begun in 1978, this is a vibrant, adventuresome and avant-garde theatre group. In addition to the theatre program, Seven Stages also sponsors literary arts activities, dance, music, and visual arts. Seven Stages has sponsored an impressive set of authors-in-residence, including Allen Ginsberg, Michael McClure, Diane Wakowski, Steven Kent and others.

14 Theatre Gael. Performances are held at the 14th St. Playhouse, 14th St. and Juniper, Midtown. Call 876-1138 for reservations. Theatre Gael is one of two Celtic theatres in the United States whose mission is to preserve and promote the heritage of Ireland, Scotland and Wales. In addition to the many plays which Theatre Gael has produced, it has also hosted poetry readings, musical performances, dance, and film reviews in keeping with the focus of the theatre. One of its most popular productions, *Rab the Rhymer*, was a one-man show about the poet Robert Burns. Theatre Gael has an on-going theatre establishment in Highlands, North Carolina as well.

15 Theatre Emory. Mary Gray Munroe Theater, Dobbs University Center, Emory University Campus, 1399 Oxford Rd. N.E., 727-6187. In 1982 a unique collaboration began among experienced theater artists, scholars and students, which attracted actors, designers, and directors from the U.S. and abroad to Emory. Under the direction of these professionals, students majoring or minoring in theatre have the opportunity to train with experts, but they are allowed to assume increasing responsibility within the theatre. Plays often premiere here and the company applies an innovative approach to its productions.

16 Theatre in the Square. 11 Whitlock Ave., Marietta, 422-8369. Theatre in the Square was founded in 1982 by Michael Horne and Palmer Wells, who continue to serve as producing artistic director and managing director, respectively. Cobb County's first professional theatre has certainly attracted a lot of support from Atlantans who are more than willing to make the drive to historic Marietta for the variety of quality productions this theatre has to offer. Theatregoers arrive at a Victorian music hall facade and proceed into an open-air courtyard lobby before entering the 165-seat theatre. Seasonal offerings range from drama and comedy to historical epics. Regional and world premieres are frequently to be seen at Theatre in the Square.

17 Theatrical Outfit. 1012 Peachtree St., 872-0665. Under the direction of artistic director Eddie Levi Lee, Theatrical Outfit continues to impress Atlantans with the nature of its presentations. Begun in 1976 in a tiny theatre in the Virginia-Highlands district, Theatrical Outfit has since moved into a 200-seat facility in the Midtown area. Theatrical Outfit prides itself on producing new and evocative drama which may range from comedy and musicals to more serious work. Programming is eclectic in nature and emphasizes fusion of various styles and forms.

18 Upstairs at Gene and Gabe's. $1582^{1}/_{2}$ Piedmont Ave, 892-2261. Home of Atlanta's longest running cabaret, Upstairs at Gene and Gabe's features original musicals, comedy, and dance shows. A Second City for southern talent, the following performers all got their start here: Libby Whittemore, Megan McFarland, Theresa Dale, Victoria Tabaka and Mandy Beson. Shows start at 9 p.m., Tuesday-Saturday. Tickets range in price from $10-$16.50.

VISUAL ARTS

Reviews by Catherine Fox, Visual Arts Critic for the *Atlanta Journal-Constitution*.

19 Abstein Gallery. 558 14th St. N.W., 872-8020. Decorative paintings and sculptures by a large stable of artists are displayed in this spacious gallery. Hours: 8:30 a.m.-5:30 p.m., Monday-Friday; 10 a.m.-4 p.m., Saturday.

20 Agnes Scott College. Dalton Galleries, Dana Fine Arts Building, Agnes Scott Campus, Decatur, 371-6000. The gallery runs a program showcasing local artists as well as student and faculty exhibitions. Hours: 9 a.m.-5 p.m., Monday-Friday; 1-5 p.m, Saturday and Sunday.

21 Aliya. The Gallery of Morningside, 1402 N. Highland Ave., 892-2835. This gallery carries work in a variety of craft and fine-art media, primarily by area artists. Hours: 11 a.m.-10 p.m., Tuesday-Thursday; 11 a.m.-11 p.m., Friday and Saturday; noon-8 p.m. on Sunday.

22 Alias. TULA, 75 Bennett St., Ste. F-2, 352-3532. Gallery owner Sarah Hatch shows her work and that of regional artists in a variety of media and styles. Hours: noon-6 p.m., Wednesday and noon-5 p.m. Saturday.

23 Ann Jacob Gallery. Phipps Plaza, 3500 Peachtree Rd. N.E., 262-3399. Exhibits at this longtime Atlanta gallery include regional artists as well as such internationally known artists as Erte and Arnoldo Pomodoro. Hours: 10 a.m.-6 p.m., Monday-Saturday and by appointment. Open until 9 p.m. on Thursday.

24 Anthony Ardavian Gallery. TULA, 75 Bennett St., Ste. C-2, 352-8738. Paintings and sculpture by contemporary artists, ranging from figurative to expressionist. Hours: 10 a.m.-5 p.m., Tuesday-Saturday and by appointment.

25 Ariel Gallery. TULA, 75 Bennett St., Ste. M-2, 352-5753. A cooperative gallery of local artists, Ariel features ongoing group exhibitions of its members as well as monthly one-person shows. Hours: 11 a.m.-5 p.m., Tuesday-Saturday.

26 Artists Associates Gallery. 3261 Roswell Rd. N.E., 261-4960. This gallery features ongoing group exhibitions of member artists as well as one-person shows. Hours: 10 a.m.-5 p.m., Tuesday-Saturday.

27 The Arts Connection. 360 Pharr Rd., 237-0005. More like a shop than a gallery, The Arts Connection shows primarily regional artists of all stripes and price ranges. Hours: 9 a.m.-10 p.m., daily.

28 ArtSpace. Hurt Building, 50 Hurt Plaza, Ste. 150, 577-1988. Art consultant Dottie McCrae shows a mix of crafts and fine arts at this downtown gallery. Hours: 9 a.m.-6 p.m., Monday-Friday. By appointment on weekends.

29 ArtVue. East Village Square, 220 Pharr Rd., 841-9130. Variety characterizes this gallery's offerings. Hours: 11 a.m.-6 p.m., Tuesday-Friday; 1 p.m.-6 p.m., Saturday and Sunday.

30 Atlanta Artists Club. 2927 Grandview Ave. N.E., 237-2324. The club exhibits watercolors, pastels, paintings, and sculpture by member artists. Hours: 10 a.m.-4 p.m., Thursday-Friday; 1-4 p.m., Saturday.

31 Atlanta Art Gallery. 262 E. Paces Ferry Rd., 261-1233. Specializing in nineteenth- and twentieth-century American and European paintings. Hours: 10:30 a.m.-5:30 p.m., Monday-Saturday.

32 Atlanta College of Art. Memorial Arts Building, Woodruff Arts Center, 1280 Peachtree St. N.E., 898-1157. One of the important non-profit galleries in Atlanta, it focuses on contemporary art, often organizing provocative, themed group exhibitions. Hours: 10 a.m.-5 p.m., Monday-Saturday; 1-6 p.m., Sunday.

33 Atlanta Photography Gallery. 495 Peachtree St. N.E., 881-8139. This non-profit gallery brings in exhibitions of notable photographers and showcases local talent. Hours: 11 a.m.-4 p.m., Wednesday-Saturday.

34 Axis Twenty Inc. 200 Peachtree Hills Ave., 261-4022. High-style furniture by craftsmen from around the country and other contemporary decorative arts are the purview of this gallery. Hours: 9 a.m.-5 p.m., Monday-Friday; 11 a.m.-4 p.m., Saturday.

35 Berman Gallery. 1131 Euclid Ave. N.E., 525-2529. Ceramics, much of it functional, is the gallery's mainstay, but it also represents famed visionary the Rev. Howard Finster and other folk artists as well as occasionally offering contemporary art exhibits in other media. Hours: 10 a.m.-5:30 p.m., Tuesday-Saturday.

36 Callanwolde Fine Arts Center. 980 Briarcliff Rd. N.E., 872-5338. The Candler (Coca-Cola) mansion, Callanwolde is a reliable venue for emerging local artists, and the beauty of the building and grounds is additional justification for making a visit. Hours: 10 a.m.-3 p.m., Monday-Saturday.

37 Carlson and Lobrano Gallery. 55 Bennett St., 351-9897. Folk art is one of the specialties here. Hours: 10 a.m.-6 p.m., Monday-Saturday.

38 Center for Puppetry Arts . 1404 Spring St. N.W., 873-3089. See **ATTRACTIONS, Family and Children's Activities.**

39 Chastain Arts Center. 135 W. Wieuca Rd., 257-1804 or 257-1747. This city-operated gallery specializes in (but is not limited to) crafts. Hours: 1-5 p.m. Wednesday-Saturday.

40 Connell Gallery/Great American. 333 Buckhead Ave., 261-1712. This top-flight crafts gallery shows contemporary expressions in fiber, glass, wood, metal, and clay. Hours: 10 a.m.-5 p.m. Monday-Saturday.

41 Deanne Levinson American Antiques. 2995 Lookout Place, 264-0106. Count on finding very fine examples of eighteenth- and early-nineteenth-century American furniture at the shop of the discerning Ms. Levinson. She also offers seventeenth- and eighteenth-century ceramics and brass and Southern folk art. Hours: 10 a.m.-4 p.m. Monday-Friday; 9 a.m.-noon on Saturday.

42 Emory University Museum of Art and Archaeology. Michael C. Carlos Hall, Main Quadrangle, near the intersection of North Decatur and Oxford roads, 727-7522. See **ATTRACTIONS. Libraries and Museums**.

43 Eve Mannes Gallery. TULA, 75 Bennett St., Ste. A., 351-6651. Elegance and craftsmanship link the artists working in crafts and fine-arts media whose work is displayed here. The gallery lineup leans toward artists of national stature, but includes accomplished regional artists, too. Hours: 9:30 a.m.-5:30 p.m. Monday-Friday and 11 a.m.-5 p.m. Saturday.

VISUAL ARTS

44 Fay Gold Gallery. 247 Buckhead Ave., 233-3843. This gallery has built a reputation for offering some of the most provocative and trendy contemporary art in the city. It is also one of the few to regularly exhibit photography. Hours: 9:30 a.m.-5:30 p.m. Monday-Friday; 10 a.m.-5:30 p.m. Saturday.

45 Framers on Fourteenth. 194 14th St. N.W., 892-1271. Featuring large multimedia exhibitions including work in fiber, wood, clay and paint. Hours: 10 a.m.-6 p.m. Monday-Friday; 11 a.m.-5 p.m. Saturday.

46 Gallery at CNN Center. Upper level of atrium, Techwood Dr. and Marietta St., 827-1825. Storefront exhibitions of regional artists. Hours: 8 a.m.-6 p.m. daily.

47 Georgia State University Art Gallery. Peachtree Center Avenue at Gilmer St., 651-3424. The art faculty's diverse interests are reflected in the variety of the exhibition schedule, which can range from Japanese metalsmithing to contemporary fiber art. Student and faculty shows are also regular presentations. Hours: 8 a.m.-8 p.m. weekdays.

48 Georgia Tech Student Center Gallery. Fred B. Wenn Student Center, Georgia Tech Campus, 350 Ferst Dr. N.W., 894-2805. Local artists are this gallery's mainstay. Hours: 10 a.m.-4 p.m. Monday-Friday; 1-5 p.m. Saturday and Sunday.

49 Goethe Institute. 400 Colony Square, 892-2388. The Institute brings in traveling exhibitions of German artists and features one-person shows of local artists who have some connection to Germany. Hours: 11 a.m.-6 p.m. Monday-Thursday; 11 a.m.-2 p.m. Saturday. Closed Friday.

50 Hammonds House Galleries and Resource Center. 503 Peeples St. S.W., 752-8215. The spirit of the late art collector Otis T. Hammonds lives on in his Victorian home.

Fulton County purchased Hammonds' estate, including his collection of African-American and Haitian art, in order to start a gallery devoted to black artists. The first floor houses changing exhibitions. An archive and library occupy the second floor. Hours: 10 a.m.-6 p.m. Tuesday-Friday; 1-5 p.m. Saturday and Sunday.

51 Heath Gallery. 416 E. Paces Ferry Rd., 262-6407. This longtime gallery has built a stable of fine regional and nationally known artists whose work fits into a sensibility leaning toward (though not limited to) minimal and conceptual art. Ceramic sculpture by such luminaries as Jun Kaneko and Margie Hughto has been a strong suit. Hours: 11 a.m.-5 p.m. Tuesday-Saturday.

52 High Museum of Art. 1280 Peachtree St. N.E., 892-4444. See **ATTRACTIONS. Libraries and Museums.**

53 High Museum of Art at Georgia-Pacific Center. 133 Peachtree St. N.E., 577-6940. See **ATTRACTIONS. Libraries and Museums**.

54 Hughley Gallery & Objects. 142 Stovall St., 523-3201. African-American artists are the focus of the neighborhood gallery. Hours: noon-5 p.m. Wednesday-Friday; 1-5 p.m. Saturday; 3-5 p.m. Sunday.

55 Jackson Fine Art. 515 E. Paces Ferry Rd., 233-3739. The only commercial gallery devoted to photography, Jackson offers prints by the acknowledged masters as well as the talented artists of the Southeast. Hours: 10 a.m.-6 p.m. Tuesday-Saturday.

56 Lagerquist Gallery. 3235 Paces Ferry Place N.W., 261-8273. Lagerquist offers both representational and abstract two- and three-dimensional work whose disparate imagery is linked by gentleness and gentility. Hours: 10:30 a.m.-5 p.m. Tuesday-Saturday.

⑤⑦ The Lowe Gallery. TULA, 75 Bennett St., Ste. A-2. 352-8114. One of the largest galleries in town, Lowe specializes in figurative art of a psychological bent, but offers abstractions, too. Hours: 10:30 a.m.-5:30 p.m. Tuesday-Friday; noon-5 p.m. Saturday.

⑤⑧ Mac Gallery. 1479 Spring St., 881-6074. This gallery takes an eclectic approach, focusing on crafts and decorative arts made by artists all over the country. Owner Jill Van Tosh's flair for the dramatic is evident from the variety — jewelry and lighting to old weather vanes — on display. Hours: by appointment only.

⑤⑨ Marietta/Cobb Museum of Art. 30 Atlanta St. N.E., Marietta, 424-8142. See **ATTRACTIONS. Libraries and Museums.**

⑥⓪ McIntosh Gallery. 1 Virginia Hill, 587 Virginia Ave N.E., 892-4023. The gallery focuses on contemporary art and includes Jacob Lawrence in its stable. Hours: 11 a.m.-5 p.m. Tuesday-Saturday.

⑥① New Visions Gallery. Lobby of the First Union Building, 999 Peachtree St. N.E., 874-3881. A non-profit gallery founded to showcase the community's emerging and midcareer artists. Also traveling exhibitions of local interest. Hours: 10 a.m.-5 p.m. Tuesday-Friday; noon-5 p.m. Saturday.

⑥② Nexus Galleries. 535 Means St., 688-2500. Dedicated to cutting-edge art in all media, Nexus' capacious gallery favors the provocative over the pretty. Its non-profit status enables it to support risk-taking and experimental expression. Nexus also supports a press that publishes artists' books whose variety and imaginativeness certainly warrant a visit to the Press' digs. Hours: 11 a.m.-5 p.m. Tuesday-Saturday.

⑥③ Oglethorpe University. 4484 Peachtree Rd. N.E., 261-1441. Offbeat and unpredictable offerings, from Japanese calligraphy to forensic sculpture. Hours: call for hours.

VISUAL ARTS

64 Peachtree Gallery. 2277 Peachtree Rd. N.E., 355-0511. Specializing in late nineteenth- and early twentieth-century paintings and works on paper. Hours: 10 a.m.-5 p.m. Monday-Saturday.

65 Sandler Hudson Gallery. 1831-A Peachtree Rd. N.E., 350-8480. This small but architecturally sophisticated space showcases some of the best emerging talent in the Southeast. Hours: 10 a.m.-5 p.m. Tuesday-Friday; noon-5 p.m. Saturday; also by appointment.

66 Schatten Gallery. Robert W. Woodruff Library, Emory Campus. 727-6861. Offering a variety of fine art and historical exhibits. Hours: 8 a.m.-midnight Monday-Thursday; 8 a.m.-8 p.m. Friday; 9 a.m.-8 p.m. Saturday; 1 p.m.-midnight, Sunday.

67 Shirley Fox Gallery. 1590 Piedmont Ave. N.E., 874-7294. Offerings range from floral paintings to cells from Walt Disney's animated films. Hours: noon-6 p.m. Monday-Friday; 10 a.m.-4 p.m. Saturday.

68 The Signature Shop. 3267 Roswell Rd. N.W., 237-4426. The oldest extant craft gallery in the country, the Signature Shop features craftwork both functional and non-functional, selected by the demanding eye of owner Blanche Reeves. Hours: 9:30 a.m.-5 p.m. Monday-Friday; 10 a.m.-5 p.m. Saturday.

69 Southeastern Center for Photographic Arts. 1935 Cliff Valley Way N.E., Ste. 210, 633-1990. The gallery schedule is divided between faculty and student shows and exhibits of photographers from around the country. Hours: 8:30 a.m.-5 p.m. Monday-Friday.

70 Swan Coach House Gallery. 3130 Slaton Dr. N.W., 266-2636. This gallery's varied schedule runs the gamut from Old Masters to modern art, but the emphasis is on the traditional. A portion of the proceeds from sales benefits the High Museum. Hours: 10 a.m.-4 p.m. Monday-Saturday.

VISUAL ARTS

71 Trinity Gallery. 249 Trinity Ave., 525-7546. An urban pioneer, this contemporary gallery is housed in a high-ceilinged, renovated building. Hours: 10 a.m.-5 p.m. Monday-Friday; 11 a.m.-4 p.m. Saturday; also by appointment.

72 Vespermann Glass Gallery. 2140 Peachtree Rd., Ste. 240, 350-9698. **Vespermann Craft Gallery.** 2140 Peachtree Rd., Ste. 237, 350-9545. **Vespermann Corporate Show Room.** 2140 Peachtree Rd., warehouse behind galleries, 350-9676. Vespermann Glass Gallery features museum-quality glass from artists around the country. The Craft Gallery handles American-crafted handicraft items in mixed media. Gifts for business or art for the corporate world can be found in the Corporate Show Room. Hours: 9 a.m.-5 p.m. Monday-Saturday. Open until 7 p.m. on Thursday.

RESTAURANTS

Atlanta has become a restaurant town. Top chefs and restaurateurs are known by their first names, and the debut of a bistro is more eagerly awaited than opening night at the symphony. When a restaurant or menu fails to measure up, Atlantans go elsewhere instantly, because there's always something new.

In this selective guide, recommended restaurants are ranked by price per person (including drinks where appropriate), with $ representing a full meal under $10, $$ from $10 to $25 and $$$ over $25. Within each category, the quality of food and comfort is rated from "A" to "D." The 10 best restaurants in the city are noted with the symbol ★. Restaurants that serve late (until at least 11 p.m.) are noted with the symbol ●. — Elliott Mackle

Cuisine Index

CUISINE INDEX

★ – denotes "Top 10" selection
● – denotes open late

CUISINE INDEX

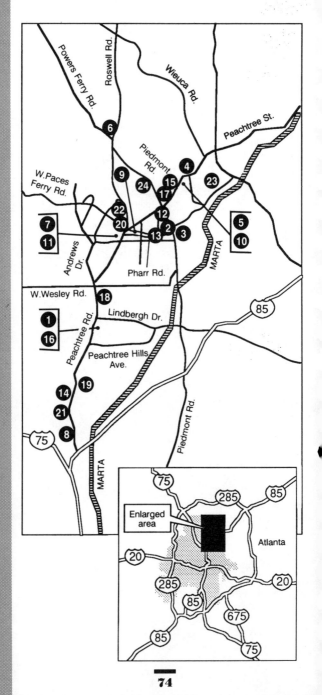

BUCKHEAD

Dining at a Glance

Map	Fare	Attire	Cost
1 Abruzzi	Italian	Dressy	$$$
2 Bone's	Steak	Dressy	$$$
3 Buckhead Diner	American	Dressy	$$$
4 The Cafe	Continental	Dressy	$$$
4 The Dining Room	Haute	Very Dressy	$$$
5 California Pizza Kitchen	Italian	Casual	$$
6 Carbo's Cafe	Continental	Dressy	$$$
7 Chops	Steaks	Dressy	$$$
8 Coach & Six	American	Dressy	$$$
9 East Village Grille	American	Informal	$$
10 The Fish Market	Seafood	Dressy	$$$
11 Frogs	Continental	Dressy	$$
12 Grill Room at McKinnon's	American	Informal	$$
13 Hedgerose Heights Inn	Haute	Very dressy	$$$
14 Houston's	American	Casual	$
15 Hsu's Gourmet Chinese	Chinese	Dressy	$$$
16 Jim White's Halfshell	Seafood	Informal	$$
17 Kamogawa	Far East	Very dressy	$$$
18 La Grotta	Italian	Very dressy	$$$
19 Longhorn Steaks	Steak	Casual	$$
20 103 West	Continental	Dressy	$$$
21 R. Thomas' Deluxe Grill	Short Order	Casual	$$
22 Rio Bravo Cantina	Mexican	Casual	$$
23 Ruth's Chris Steakhouse	Steak	Informal	$$$
24 Trio	American	Dressy	$$$

KEY: $-full meal under $10; $$-from $10-$25; $$$-more than $25

❶ Abruzzi Ristorante. 2355 Peachtree Rd. (Peachtree Battle Shopping Center), 261-8186. Italian. If you're rich, pampered and live in Genoa, Milan, New York, or Atlanta, this is the kind of unabashedly upscale yet informal place you prefer. Cuisine is reassuringly authentic yet always amusing. The reasonably priced wine card is among the strongest Italian lists in the city. Choice: penne with four cheeses, veal piccata, deep-fried zucchini and pears in red wine. Food/ A. Comfort/A. Dressy. $$$. Lunch Monday-Friday, dinner Monday-Saturday. Reservations and all major credit cards accepted.

❷ Bone's ★ •. 3130 Piedmont Rd. N.E. 237-2663. Steak and Seafood. Clubby atmosphere, prime beef and fresh seafood, conventional service for macho movers and shakers. Choice: steak, prime rib. Dressy. $$$. Food/A. Comfort/B. Lunch weekdays, dinner until 11 p.m. daily. Cigar smoking allowed. Credit cards, reservations, valet parking.

❸ Buckhead Diner ★ •. 3073 Piedmont Rd. N.E., 262-3336. American. Sleek and chic, the town's most luxurious snack shop provides fun food for high rollers. Choice: salt-and-pepper squid, grilled stuffed pasilla pepper. Dressy. $$$. Food/A. Comfort/B. Lunch and dinner daily. Major Credit cards, valet parking, no reservations.

❹ The Cafe •. The Dining Room ★. The Ritz-Carlton, Buckhead, 3434 Peachtree Rd., 237-2700. Hotel-continental; haute cuisine. The downstairs Cafe is charming, with adequate food and good service. The upstairs Dining Room, Atlanta's best restaurant, features a dizzying succession of inventive dishes by chef Gunter Seeger, superior service and wine list, British baronial atmosphere. Menu changes daily. The Cafe choice: spa cuisine selection. Dressy. $$$. Food/B. Comfort/A. The Dining Room choice: Chef Seeger's handwritten daily menu with selection of wines. Very dressy. $$$. Food/A. Comfort/A. Cafe: breakfast, lunch and dinner daily. The Dining

Room: dinner nightly except Sundays. Major credit cards, reservations.

⑤ California Pizza Kitchen. 3393 Peachtree Rd. N.E., (Lenox Square), 262-9221. Designer pizza. Los Angeles mall-food import; highly mannered mix of shiny surfaces, determinedly perky service, unusual flattops—shrimp pesto, Thai chicken, like that. Choice: vegetarian pizza. Casual. $$. Food/B. Comfort/C. Open daily. Major credit cards.

⑥ Carbo's Cafe. 3717 Roswell Rd., 231-4162. Continental. Traditional, upscale dining with music, mahogany bar. Choice: oyster pesto. Dressy. $$$. Food/B. Comfort/B. Dinner nightly. Major credit cards, reservations, open late.

⑦ Chops. 70 West Paces Ferry Rd. at Peachtree Rd., 262-2675. Steaks. Atlanta's new temple of post-modern conspicuous consumption is loud, smoky, physically irritating and wildly popular. Beef is prime, corn-fed stuff from the Midwest, flawlessly prepared. Grilled lamb chops and salmon, smoked pork chops, crab cakes, fried shrimp and vegetables are good, too. Save room for lemon tart and chocolate chip butterscotch pie. Choice: ribeye steak. Dressy. $$$. Food/A. Comfort/C. Lunch Mondays-Fridays; dinner nightly. Reservations, major credit cards, valet parking; not wheelchair friendly.

⑧ Coach & Six. 1776 Peachtree Rd. (Brookwood), 872-6666. American. Clubby, brass-and-banquette dining room for bankers and brokers; snob-appeal atmosphere, food more 1950s than 1990s.
Choice: veal chop, filet mignon, chocolate velvet. Dressy. $$$. Food/B. Comfort/A. Lunch weekdays. Dinner nightly. Menus in five languages. Major credit cards, reservations, valet parking.

⑨ East Village Grill •. 248 Buckhead Ave. N.E., 233-3345. American. Firehouse transformed into hot singles bar with comfort-food menu. Choice: grilled chicken breast. Informal. $$. Food/B. Comfort/C. Lunch and dinner daily. Major credit cards; not wheelchair accessible.

⑩ The Fish Market •. 3393 Peachtree Rd. N.E. (Lenox Square), 262-3165. Seafood. Swanky fish house tucked into the basement of a food court. Choice: crabcakes. Dressy. $$$. Food/B. Comfort/B. Lunch and dinner daily except Sundays. Major credit cards, reservations, valet parking.

⑪ Frogs: A Bistro. 68 West Paces Ferry Rd., 261-2299. Continental. The Frenchified food at this cleverly gotten up watering hole is at once prosaic and arresting: ham hocks, lamb shanks, thick soups, and dramatic-looking desserts. The room is loud enough to pop eardrums. Choice: chicken hash with chunky tomato sauce. Dressy. $$. Food/B. Comfort/C. Lunch and dinner daily. Major credit cards, reservations for six or more, complimentary valet parking; not wheelchair friendly.

⑫ The Grill Room at McKinnon's •. 3209 Maple Dr. (at Peachtree Rd.), 237-1313. American. Reverse-chic Pan-American bistro within a larger, much fancier Cajun-Creole restaurant. Choice: Chicken Yucatan style, grilled seafood. Informal. $$. Food/B. Comfort/B. Dinner nightly except Sundays. Major credit cards; no reservations.

⑬ Hedgerose Heights Inn ★. 490 E. Paces Ferry Rd., 233-7673. Haute cuisine. Luxury dining, generally considered the city's leading independent restaurant—and the most formal. Choice: wild game. Very dressy. $$$. Food/A. Comfort/A. Dinner Tuesdays-Saturdays. Major credit cards, reservations.

⑭ Houston's. 2166 Peachtree Rd., 351-2442. Clever, casual grill fare is featured at this locally-based chain's three Atlanta units. Loud and lively, they're designed for yups and younger. Though a wait is usually necessary at peak hours, service is swift once you sit down. Choice: the burger. Casual. $ Food/B. Comfort/B. Lunch and dinner daily. Major credit cards, no reservations.

15 Hsu's Gourmet Chinese. 3340 Peachtree Rd. N.E. (Tower Place), 233-3891. Cantonese. Elegant, beautifully decorated series of rooms. Exquisite food, presentation. Choice: stuffed lettuce, fried rice (best in town). Dressy. $$$. Food/A. Comfort/B. Lunch weekdays and dinner nightly except Sundays. Major credit cards, reservations.

16 Jim White's Halfshell. 2349 Peachtree Rd. N.E. (Peachtree Battle Shopping Center), 237-9924. Seafood. Shells, nets, mounted sailfish, motherly servers—every city has its old, familiar seafood restaurant. Choice: scampi. Informal. $$. Food/C. Comfort/C. Dinner nightly except Sundays. Major credit cards.

17 Kamogawa. Hotel Nikko Atlanta, 3300 Peachtree Rd. at Piedmont, 841-0314. Japanese. The city's most elegant and expensive Oriental restaurant is worth every yen. Extraordinary food and sublime service are shaking up the Buckhead fine dining scene. Choice: kaiseki dinner in a tatami room. Very dressy. $$$. Food/A. Comfort/A. Lunch and dinner daily. Major credit cards, valet parking.

18 La Grotta Ristorante Italiano ★. 2637 Peachtree Rd. N.E. (Peachtree House), 231-1368. Northern Italian. Suave continental service, to-order food, reliable. Choice: homemade pasta. Very dressy. $$$. Food/A. Comfort/B. Dinner Monday-Saturday. Major credit cards; reservations, valet parking.

19 Longhorn Steaks •. 2151 Peachtree Rd. N.E., 351-6086. Texan. First in a fast-growing local chain with Skeeter's Mesquite Grilles part of the family. Choice: ribeye steak. Casual. $$. Food/B. Comfort/C. Lunch and dinner. Major credit cards; no reservations.

20 103 West ★ •. 103 W. Paces Ferry Rd. N.W., 233-5993. Continental. Amusingly overdecorated series of luxurious rooms. Setting can make you forget the wonderfully inventive food. Choice: sauteed sweetbreads. Dressy. $$$. Food/A. Comfort/A. Dinner nightly except Sundays. Major credit cards, reservations, valet parking; not wheelchair friendly.

㉑ R. Thomas' Deluxe Grill •. 1812 Peachtree Rd. N.W. (Brookwood), 872-2942. Short orders. Decorated to resemble a Hollywood trivia-buff's closet, features an eclectic menu of fresh and wholesome novelties. Choice: shrimp omelet on the patio. Casual. $$. Food/B. Comfort/ C. Open for breakfast, lunch and dinner daily. Major credit cards; no reservations.

㉒ Rio Bravo Cantina. 3172 Roswell Rd., 262-7431. Tex-Mex. Food and decor are make-believe Mexican; fun if you take nothing seriously. Choice: beef fajitas. Casual. $$. Food/B. Comfort/ C. Lunch and dinner daily.

㉓ Ruth's Chris Steakhouse. 950 E. Paces Ferry Rd. (Atlanta Plaza), 365-0660. Steaks. Branch of the New Orleans original, features prime, hand-cut beef. Choice: grilled steaks and fish. Informal. $$$. Food/B. Comfort/B. Lunch weekdays, dinner nightly. Major credit cards, reservations.

㉔ Trio. 3402 Piedmont Rd. N.E., 231-8740. California. Big, black-and-white art-deco supper club, a cross between El Morocco and Banana Republic. Attractive staff, good wine list, unusual food. Choice: grilled tuna with wasabe sauce, milk-chocolate cheesecake. Dressy. $$$. Food/B. Comfort/B. Lunch and dinner daily except no lunch on Saturdays. Major credit cards, valet parking; no reservations.

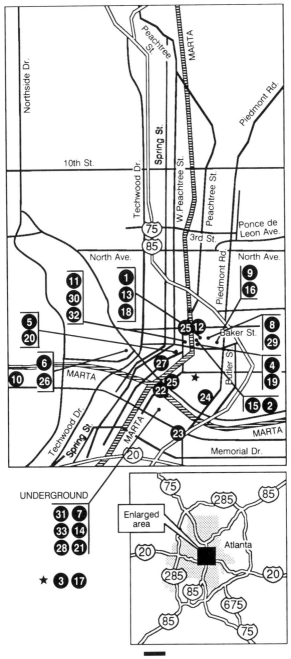

UNDERGROUND

81

DOWNTOWN

Dining at a Glance

Map		Fare	Attire	Cost
1	Avanzare	Italian	Informal	$$$
2	The Cafe	Continental	Informal	$$
2	The Restaurant	Continental	Dressy	$$$
3	City Grill	Seafood	Dressy	$$$
4	Dailey's	American	Informal	$$$
5	Delectables	American	Informal	$
6	The Great Wall	Chinese	Informal	$$
7	Lombardi's	Italian	Informal	$$
8	Morton's of Chicago	Steak	Informal	$$
9	Nikolai's Roof	Russian	Dressy	$$$
10	Paschal's	Southern	Informal	$
11	Savannah Fish Company	Seafood	Dressy	$$$
Downtown Lunch				
12	American Lunch	Southern	Casual	$
14	Barker's Famous Hot Dogs	Short order	Casual	$
16	Cafe de la Paix	Buffet	Informal	$$
18	Clock of 5's	American	Informal	$$
21	E. 48th St. Market	Italian	Casual	$
22	First Atlanta Cafeteria	Self-serve	Informal	$
23	State Employees Cafeteria	Self-serve	Informal	$
24	Georgia State University	Self-serve	Informal	$
25	Gorin's	Short order	Casual	$
27	Il Cappuccino Cafe	Italian	Informal	$
31	Southern Vittles	American	Informal	$
32	Sun Dial	Continental	Informal	$$
33	Turkey Express	Southern	Casual	$

KEY: $-full meal under $10; $$-from $10-$25; $$$-more than $25

1 Avanzare. Hyatt Regency Atlanta, 265 Peachtree St., 577-1234. Contemporary Italian. Bright tile, large saltwater aquarium and pasta bar are features of the hotel's revamped specialty dining room. Choice: chocolate desserts. Informal to dressy. Food/C. Comfort/B. $$$. Lunch weekdays; dinner nightly. Major credit cards, reservations, valet parking.

2 The Cafe ● . The Restaurant. The Ritz-Carlton, Atlanta, 181 Peachtree St., 659-0400. Haute hotel-continental. Good food upstairs and down, with dress code a bit less stringent in The Cafe below. Both rooms plush, culinary standards very high. Cafe choice: prix fixe menu. Informal. $$. Food/B. Comfort/B. Restaurant choice: desserts. Dressy. $$$. Food/B. Comfort/A. Cafe open for breakfast, lunch and dinner nightly and open late. The Restaurant is open for lunch Monday-Friday, Sunday brunch and dinner nightly. Major credit cards, reservations, valet parking.

3 City Grill. 50 Hurt Plaza, facing Central City Park, 524-2489. Seafood. Lush, plush and ultra-clubby, this ocean liner of a restaurant is downtown's best bet for perfectly-cooked fish. The chef is young and savvy, the service smart, the wine list tops, the whole operation improving every day. Choice: hot smoked Irish salmon. Dressy. Food/A. Comfort/B. $$$. Lunch weekdays; dinner nightly. Cigar smoking allowed. Reservations and all major credit cards, valet parking at night. Not wheelchair friendly so call ahead for directions.

4 Dailey's. 17 International Blvd. N.E., 681-3303. American. Local Peasant chain's unit aimed at out-of-towners. Rehabbed warehouse setting a lot more dramatic than the ho-hum food. Choice: steak. Informal. $$$. Food/C. Comfort/B. Lunch and dinner daily. Major credit cards.

5 Delectables ★. Lower level, Atlanta-Fulton Public Library Central Branch, One Margaret Mitchell Square (outdoor entrance corner of Carnegie Way and Fairlie St.), 681-2909. American Modern pastel-and-wood cafe serving homemade pastries and light luncheon items. Choice: quiche, raspberry-almond tart in the courtyard. Informal. $. Food/A. Comfort/B. Lunch weekdays. Convenient for takeout. No major credit cards.

6 The Great Wall. Street level, CNN Center, One Omni International, 522-8213. Chinese. Food nothing special, but service is quick and the place is convenient. Choice: Kung Pao Shrimp. Informal. $$. Food/C. Comfort/C. Lunch and dinner. Major credit cards.

7 Lombardi's Underground. Underground Atlanta, 94 Upper Pryor St., Ste. 239, 522-6568. Italian. Arguably the best sit-down food in Underground Atlanta. The dining space is picture pretty but loud, service generally swift and pleasant, if slightly goofy. Choice: all pastas, including cannelloni stuffed with minced veal and spinach, with two sauces. Informal. Food/B. Comfort/B. $$. Lunch weekdays; dinner every night. All major credit cards, reservations.

8 Morton's of Chicago •. 245 Peachtree Center Ave. (Marquis One Tower), 577-4366. Steaks. Brash, boisterous grill catering to big spenders, often too loud for conversation. Top quality beef. Choice: Porterhouse steak. Informal to dressy. $$$. Food/B. Comfort/B. Lunch weekdays, dinner daily. Major credit cards, reservations before 7 p.m., valet parking at night.

9 Nikolai's Roof. Hilton Hotel, 255 Courtland St. N.E., 659-2000. Russian. Dramatic views of the city from this small, exclusive room. Czarist atmosphere and menu an amusing fantasy. Choice: pirozkis, hot souffles. Dressy. $$$. Food/B. Comfort/A. Dinner only, two sittings. Major credit cards, reservations required, valet parking.

⑩ Paschal's. 830 Martin Luther King, Jr., Dr., 577-3150. Southern. Slightly down-at-the-heels motel, a major meeting ground for the black community. Good, caring service and soul food.Choice: fried pork chop, chicken-liver omelet. Informal. $. Food/C. Comfort/C. Lunch and dinner daily. Major credit cards; no reservations.

⑪ Savannah Fish Company •. Westin Peachtree Plaza Hotel, Peachtree St. at International Blvd., 589-7456. Seafood. Fresh seafood prepared to order amid fountains and Japanese banners. Choice: Savannah fish stew. Dressy. $$$. Food/B. Comfort/B. Lunch and dinner daily. Major credit cards, valet parking.

DOWNTOWN LUNCH

From cellars to rooftops, grand luxe to stand-up, Atlanta's downtown lunch scene is varied and amusing. The more formal spots accept reservations, which will generally be held no more than 15 minutes. It is always best to call and inquire before going to a particular restaurant.

⑫ American Lunch. Mall level, Food Court, Peachtree Center, 230 Peachtree St., 688-2887. Southern takeout. Hot and cold buffet items are self-serve and priced by the ounce. Seating in the adjacent common eating spaces can be tight at noontime. Choice: fried chicken livers, mashed potatoes, casseroles. Come as you are. $. Food/B. Comfort/D. Breakfast and lunch Monday-Friday and lunch on Saturdays.

⑬ Avanzare. Hyatt Regency Atlanta, 265 Peachtree St., 577-1234. Contemporary Italian. Bright tile, large saltwater aquarium and pasta bar are features of the hotel's revamped specialty dining room. Choice: chocolate desserts. Food/C. Comfort/B. $$. Lunch weekdays. Major credit cards, reservations, valet parking.

⑭ Barker's Famous Hot Dogs. Food Court, Underground Atlanta. Frankfurters. Accept no substitutes. The dogs, imported from New York, are cooked over charcoal and pug-ugly. Choice: white dog. Food/B. Comfort/C. $.

⑮ The Cafe, The Restaurant. The Ritz-Carlton, Atlanta, 181 Peachtree St., 659-0400. Haute hotel-continental. Good food upstairs and down, with dress code a bit less stringent in The Cafe below. Both rooms plush, culinary standards very high. Cafe choice: prix fixe menu. Informal. $$. Food/B. Comfort/B. Restaurant choice: lobster club sandwich. A luxurious buffet lunch, served weekdays in the Restaurant's bar area, represents the best value downtown. Dressy. $$. Food/B. Comfort/A. Cafe open for lunch daily. The Restaurant is open for lunch Monday-Friday, brunch Sundays. Major credit cards, reservations, valet parking.

⑯ Cafe de la Paix. Atlanta Hilton, Courtland and Harris Sts., 659-2000, ext. 1594. Buffet. Lavish selection of hot and cold items in a bright and charming setting. Choice: buffet. Informal. $$. Food/C. Comfort/B. Lunch weekdays, brunch Sundays. Reservations, major credit cards, valet parking.

⑰ City Grill. 50 Hurt Plaza, facing Central City Park, 524-2489. Seafood. Lush, plush and ultra-clubby, this ocean liner of a restaurant is downtown's best bet for perfectly-cooked fish. The chef is young and savvy, the service smart, the wine list tops, the whole operation improving every day. Choice: hot smoked Irish salmon. Dressy. Food/A. Comfort/B. $$$. Lunch weekdays; dinner nightly. Cigar smoking allowed. Reservations, all major credit cards, valet parking at night. Not wheelchair friendly so call ahead for directions.

DOWNTOWN LUNCH

86

⑱ Clock of 5's. Hyatt Regency Atlanta, 265 Peachtree St., 577-1234. American grill. Handsome midprice room featuring sandwiches, salads. Often packed at lunch. Choice: low-calorie spa menu. Informal. $$. Food/B. Comfort/B. Lunch weekdays. Major credit cards.

⑲ Dailey's. 17 International Blvd. N.E., 681-3303. American. Local Peasant chain's unit aimed at out-of-towners. Rehabbed warehouse setting a lot more dramatic than the ho-hum food. Choice: fruit salad. Informal. $$$. Food/C. Comfort/B. Lunch and dinner daily. Major credit cards.

⑳ Delectables. Lower level, Atlanta-Fulton Public Library Central Branch, One Margaret Mitchell Square (outdoor entrance corner of Carnegie Way and Fairlie St.), 681-2909. American Modern pastel-and-wood cafe serving homemade pastries and light luncheon items. Choice: quiche, raspberry-almond tart in the courtyard. Informal. $. Food/A. Comfort/B. Lunch weekdays. Convenient for takeout. No major credit cards.

㉑ E. 48th Street Market. Lower Alabama Street, opposite Food Court, Underground Atlanta. Italian. Sandwiches to satisfy the most demanding, ravenous hunger. Pastas, pastries and minimal groceries as well at this branch of a Dunwoody store. Choice: eggplant parmigiana hero with tomato sauce and homemade mozzarella. Casual. $. Food/B. Comfort/C. Continuous service daily. No table service. Open late Fridays and Saturdays. Good for carry out.

㉒ First Atlanta Cafeteria. Second floor, 2 Peachtree St., 332-6388. Steam table. Bank-subsidized operation for employees offers better than average food at reasonable prices. Nice view. Choice: fried chicken, baked fish, vegetables. Informal. Food/B. Comfort/C. $. Lunch weekdays.

㉓ Georgia State Employees Cafeteria.
Floyd Twin Towers, 2 Martin Luther King, Jr.,
Dr., 656-2606. Unimaginative cooking not a
proper reflection of Georgia's agricultural bounty.
Choice: baked chicken, strawberry shortcake.
Informal. Food/C. Comfort/B. $. Lunch weekdays.

㉔ Georgia State University Student Cafeterias. Third floor of Student Center, 33
Gilmer St., 658-2159. Steam table. Utilitarian student gathering place with mostly utilitarian food.
The smaller, carpeted Urban Life room is preferred. Choice: turnip greens, baked chicken.
Informal. Food/C. Comfort/C. $. Lunch weekdays.

㉕ Gorin's Homemade Ice Cream. Food
Court, Peachtree Center, 230 Peachtree St.,
525-7557; CNN Center, Omni International,
521-0588; Underground Atlanta, Upper Alabama
St., 659-4104; 620 Peachtree St., 874-0550. Dipping counters. Locally owned chain dishing out
snacks and treats. Large orders can be delivered
downtown. Choice: almond chicken melt sandwich,
bittersweet chocolate ice cream with a sprinkle of
M&Ms. Come as you are. $. Food/B. Comfort/D.

㉖ The Great Wall. Street level, CNN Center,
One Omni International, 522-8213. Chinese. Food
nothing special, but service is quick and the place
is convenient. Choice: Kung Pao Shrimp. Informal. $. Food/C. Comfort/C. Lunch. Major credit
cards.

㉗ Il Cappuccino Cafe. Healy Building lobby,
57 Forsyth St. N.W., 523-6068. Coffee house.
Small Italian-style cafe serving toasted Italian
sandwiches, salads, pastries, and coffees. Good for
takeout. Friendly. Choice: ham sandwich. Come as
you are. $. Food/C. Comfort/C.

㉘ Lombardi's Underground. Underground Atlanta, 94 Upper Pryor St., Ste. 239, 522-6568. Italian. Arguably the best sit-down food in Underground Atlanta. The dining space is picture pretty but loud, service generally swift and pleasant, if slightly goofy. Choice: all pastas, including cannelloni stuffed with minced veal and spinach, with two sauces. Informal. Food/B. Comfort/B. $$. Lunch weekdays, dinner every night. All major credit cards, reservations.

㉙ Morton's of Chicago. 245 Peachtree Center Ave. (Marquis One Tower), 577-4366. Steaks. Brash, boisterous grill catering to big spenders, often too loud for conversation. Top quality beef. Choice: hamburger. Informal to dressy. $$. Food/B. Comfort/B. Lunch weekdays. Major credit cards, reservations before 7 p.m.

㉚ Savannah Fish Company •. Westin Peachtree Plaza Hotel, Peachtree St. at International Blvd., 589-7456. Seafood. Fresh seafood prepared to order amid fountains and Japanese banners. Choice: Savannah fish stew. Dressy. $$$. Food/B. Comfort/B. Lunch daily. Major credit cards, valet parking.

㉛ Southern Vittles. Food Court, Underground Atlanta. Southern. Dixie delights: peppery, greaseless fried chicken, turnip greens, yams, cornbread muffins, peach cobbler and such. Choice: warm sweet-potato pie. Casual. $. Food/B. Comfort/C. Continuous service daily. No table service or credit cards. Open late.

㉜ Sun Dial. Top floor, Westin Peachtree Plaza Hotel, Peachtree St. at International Blvd., 659-1400. Continental. Pretend you're on Air Force One in this revolving room with a view. Choice: menu changes daily. Informal. Food/C. Comfort/B. $$. Lunch Monday-Saturday. Sunday brunch. Major credit cards, reservations.

33 Turkey Express Diner. Food Court, Underground Atlanta. Southern. Demurely seasoned, homestyle food—good value and a good place for visitors in a rush. Hot turkey sandwiches, turkey burgers, and turkey barbecue are possibilities. The staff is exceptionally cheerful, helpful and pleasant. Choice: roast turkey dinner with cornbread-sage dressing and turnip greens. Casual. $. Food/B. Comfort/C. Continuous service daily. No table service or credit cards. Open late Fridays and Saturdays. Good for carry out.

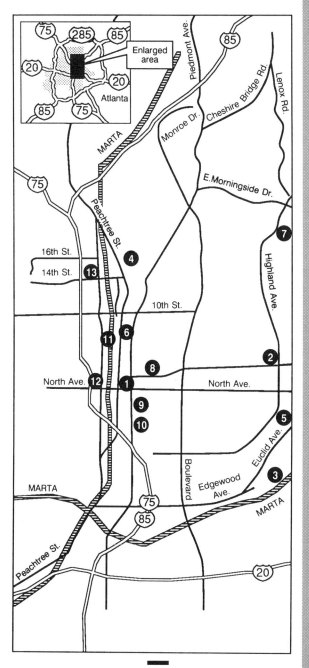

Dining at a Glance

Map	Fare	Attire	Cost
1 The Abbey	Continental	Dressy	$$$
2 Atkins Park	American	Casual	$
3 Burton's Grill	Southern	Casual	$
4 The Country Place	American	Informal	$$
5 Eat Your Vegetables	American	Casual	$
6 French Quarter Grocery	Sandwich Shop	Informal	$
7 Indigo Coastal Grill	Seafood	Informal	$$
7 Partners	American	Informal	$$
8 Mary Mac's Tea Room	Southern	Informal	$
9 Mick's	Short Order	Casual	$$
10 Pleasant Peasant	French	Informal	$$
11 Taste of New Orleans	Cajun/Creole	Informal	$$
12 The Varsity	Short Order	Casual	$
13 Veni Vidi Vici	Italian	Dressy	$$$

KEY: $-full meal under $10; $$-from $10-$25; $$$-more than $25

1 The Abbey. 163 Ponce de Leon Ave. (between Piedmont and North Ave.), 876-8532. Continental. Handsome old church turned into a slick restaurant concept—harpist in the choir loft, waiters in monkcloth, candles, clunky furniture. Pretentious menu, hit-or-miss preparation, prices are anything but heavenly. Good wine list. Choice: chocolate mousse. Dressy. $$$. Food/C. Comfort/B. Dinner nightly. Major credit cards; reservations, valet parking.

2 Atkins Park •. 794 North Highland Ave. N.E. (Poncey-Highland), 876-7249. American. Neighborhood bar-restaurant attracts a colorful, lively crowd. Convenient to nearby clubs, theaters. Choice: burgers on the patio. Casual. $. Food/C. Comfort/C. Lunch and dinner daily. Major credit cards; not wheelchair accessible.

3 Burton's Grill ★. 1029 Edgewood Ave. N.E. (Inman Park), 525-3415. Southern. Utterly simple storefront cafe in restored district; across the street from the Inman Park MARTA station. Food is cooked before your eyes, served cafeteria style,

MIDTOWN DINING

eaten at kitchen tables. Choice: fried chicken (best in town), hoecakes. Casual. $. Food/A. Comfort/D. Breakfast and lunch Monday-Saturday. No major credit cards, no alcohol, no reservations, no wheelchair access. Open early.

4 The Country Place. 1197 Peachtree St. (Midtown), 881-0144. American. Located in Colony Square, convenient to Arts Center MARTA station and Arts Center, staffed by perky young pros, this continental-country themed Peasant Corp. unit is highly popular with locals. Choice: Mile High Pie. Informal. $$. Food/C. Comfort/B. Lunch daily except Saturday; dinner nightly. Major credit cards; no reservations.

5 Eat Your Vegetables. 438 Moreland Ave., 523-2671. American. Despite its name, this is not a strictly vegetarian restaurant. No red meat, it's true, but chicken, fish, alcohol and caffeinated beverages take up the slack. Service is New Age sweet and occasionally forgetful. Daily specials include seafood, Indian, Mexican and vegetarian plates as well as complete macrobiotic meals. Choice: tofu-miso vegetable soup. Casual. $. Food/B. Comfort/C. Lunch Sunday-Friday and dinner Monday-Saturday. No smoking allowed. Mastercard, VISA, reservations for five or more.

6 French Quarter Grocery. 923 Peachtree St. (near 8th St.), 875-2489. Sandwich shop. Cajun and Creole sandwiches, bisques, plates, potato chips, New Orleans Dixie beer, Mardi Gras decor. Choice: shrimp sandwich. Informal. $. Food/B. Comfort/B. Lunch weekdays; dinner Tuesday-Saturday. Good for take out.

7 Indigo Coastal Grill and **Partners Cafe.** 1397 and 1399 North Highland Ave. (Morningside), 875-0202, 876-0676. Seafood; American. Side by side and under the same ownership, these small, crowded rooms offer witty decor, up-to-date cuisine and the atmosphere of an exclusive private party. Choice: seafood and pasta. Informal. $$. Food/B. Comfort/B. Open every night. Major credit cards; no reservations. Good for take out.

8 Mary Mac's Tea Room. 224 Ponce de Leon Ave., 874-4747. Southern. Volume lunchroom operation featuring speedy fill-ups, motherly table service. Choice: fried chicken, bran muffins, collards. Informal. $. Food/C. Comfort/C. Lunch and dinner weekdays.

9 Mick's •. 557 Peachtree St. N.E., 875-6425. Short orders. Bright lights, big-city diner (one of many Mick's around town) featuring imaginatively sauced pastas, burgers, hefty desserts. Choice: chocolate cream pie. Casual. $$. Food/B. Comfort/C. Lunch and dinner nightly. Major credit cards; no reservations; not wheelchair friendly.

10 Pleasant Peasant •. 555 Peachtree St. N.E., 874-3223. Country French. First of the highly successful Peasant chain of restaurants. Cramped, bustling with life. Choice: Scallops Parisienne. Informal. $$. Food/B. Comfort/C. Lunch Monday-Friday, dinner nightly. Major credit cards; no reservations.

11 Taste of New Orleans •. 889 W. Peachtree St. N.W. (Midtown), 874-5535. Creole and Cajun. Stylish, casual atmosphere sets off the Louisiana cooking. Choice: shrimp etouffee, red beans and rice with andouille sausage, seafood-baked eggplant. Informal. $$. Food/B. Comfort/B. Lunch Tuesday-Friday and dinner daily. Major credit cards, reservations; not wheelchair friendly.

12 The Varsity •. 61 North Ave. (at the I-75/85 Connector), 881-1706. Huge drive-in and serve-yourself snack shop, a Georgia Tech and Atlanta tradition. Customers watch television while chowing down. Choice: chili dog. Casual. $. Food/D. Comfort/C. Open daily, early to very late.

13 Veni Vidi Vici. One Atlantic Center (IBM Tower), 41 14th St., near W. Peachtree St., 875-8424. Italian. The food, based on recipes and consultation by supercook Marcella Hazan, may be the most exciting in town. The service, perhaps based on the Atlanta Falcon's play book, is among the most aggressive. Choice: lemon pasta, veal chop, lemon gelato. Dressy. $$$. Food/A. Comfort/C. Lunch weekdays, dinner nightly. Reservations, major credit cards, valet parking; not wheelchair friendly.

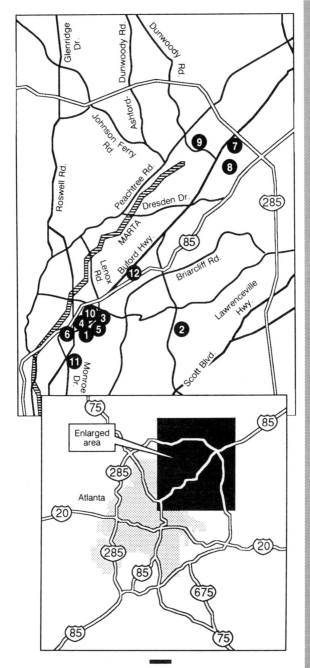

NORTHEAST

Dining at a Glance

Map		Fare	Attire	Cost
1	Abyssinia	Ethiopian	Informal	$
2	Athens Pizza House	Greek	Informal	$$
3	Bamboo Luau's Chinatown	Chinese	Informal	$$
4	Chef's Cafe	American	Informal	$$
5	Colonnade	Southern	Informal	$$
6	Don Juan	Spanish	Informal	$$
7	First China	Chinese	Informal	$$
8	Gojinka	Japanese	Informal	$$$
9	Honto	Chinese	Informal	$$
10	Marra's Seafood Grill	Seafood	Informal	$$
11	Sierra Grill	Southwestern	Informal	$$
12	Vietnamese Cuisine	Far East	Informal	$$

KEY: $-full meal under $10; $$-from $10-$25; $$$-more than $25

❶ Abyssinia •. 1803 Cheshire Bridge Rd.
N.E., 874-8450. Ethiopian. The decor is basic ethnic, the platters of spicy food delicious. Choice:
chicken in butter sauce, chilled lentils. Informal.
$. Food/B. Comfort/C. Dinner Tuesday-Sunday.
Lunch on weekends only. Major credit cards.

❷ Athens Pizza House. 1369 Clairmont Rd.,
636-1100. Greek. Original, considerably enlarged
stand in a highly successful chain. Decor is nothing, pizza all. Choice: Mediterranean Special pie.

Informal. $$. Food/B. Comfort/C. Lunch and dinner daily. Major credit cards.

3 Bamboo Luau's Chinatown •. 2263 Cheshire Bridge Rd. N.E., 636-9131. Cantonese specialties in a pink, gray, and gold setting of fish tanks and dragons. Choice: whole steamed fish, stir-fried oysters with scallions, braised watercress. Superior dim sum brunch on weekends. Informal. Food/B. Comfort/B. $$. Lunch and dinner daily. Major credit cards.

4 Chef's Cafe ★ •. 2115 Piedmont Rd. N.E. (at I-85), 872-2284. American. Clever California-style bistro, a magnet for TV and PR types. Informal. $$. Choice: crab cakes, sandwiches, pastas. Food/A. Comfort/B. Dinner daily. Major credit cards, reservations.

5 Colonnade Restaurant. 1879 Cheshire Bridge Rd., 874-5642. Southern. Here's your basic, mid-price, Dixie-menu, cloth-napkin, waitress-calls-you-Honey institution. The lengthy good-stuff list includes corn muffins, yeast rolls, roast turkey with dressing, beef tips in gravy over rice, fried chicken livers and fried oysters. The restaurant is loud and neither the staff nor the customers are as young as they once were. Choice: fried shrimp. Informal. $$. Food/B. Comfort/C. Breakfast Tuesday-Sunday, lunch and dinner everyday. Open continuously on Sunday. No reservations.

6 Don Juan. 1927 Piedmont Circle (near Piedmont Rd. at I-85), 874-4285. Friendly and romantic, Atlanta's only Spanish restaurant. Choice: white bean soup, fried squid. Informal. $$. Food/ C. Comfort/B. Lunch weekdays and dinner nightly except Sunday. Major credit cards, reservations; not wheelchair accessible.

7 First China. 5295 Buford Hwy. N.E., 457-6788. Cantonese. The Muy family keeps close watch on every (delicious) plate that leaves the kitchen. Choice: chicken with mushrooms and sausage. Informal. $$. Food/B. Comfort/C. Lunch and dinner daily. Major credit cards.

8 Gojinka. 5269 Buford Hwy. (Pinetree Shopping Center), 458-0558. Japanese. Looks-like-nothing storefront that's extremely popular with local Japanese. Choice: sashimi or sushi sampler plate. Informal. $$$. Food/A. Comfort/B. Open nightly except Sundays. Major credit cards, reservations.

9 Honto. 3295 Chamblee-Dunwoody Rd., 458-3088. Chinese. High turnover at the busy, Hong Kong-style fish house keeps the seafood selection varied and fresh. Choice: salt-and-pepper squid, steamed whole fish. Informal. $. Food/A. Comfort/C. Lunch and dinner daily. Major credit cards, reservations.

10 Marra's Seafood Grill. 1782 Cheshire Bridge Rd. N.E. (near Piedmont Rd.), 874-7347. Seafood. Fresh seafood cooked over charcoal, served in an airy wood-and-glass room. Choice: fish of the day. Informal. $$. Food/B. Comfort/B. Dinner daily. Major credit cards, reservations for large tables only, valet parking.

11 Sierra Grill. 1529 Piedmont Rd. N.E. (at Monroe Dr.), 873-5630. Modern Southwestern. Glow of the campfire, scent of the mountain pines, lots of witty Western folk art, pecks of pretty pepper. Choice: black bean soup. Informal. $$. Food/B. Comfort/B. Lunch weekdays and dinner Monday-Saturday. Major credit cards.

12 Vietnamese Cuisine. Northeast Plaza, 3375 (Ste. 1060) Buford Hwy., 321-1840. Vietnamese. Sumptuous, excellent service, food somewhat Americanized and relatively expensive. Staff speaks perfect English. A great trip, in other words. Choice: nem muong—marinated, charcoal-broiled pork meatballs served with rice paper, green vegetables and sweet, dark, coconut-based sauce. Informal. $$. Food/B. Comfort/B. Lunch and dinner Monday-Saturday. VISA and MasterCard. Restrooms not wheelchair friendly. Open very late on weekends.

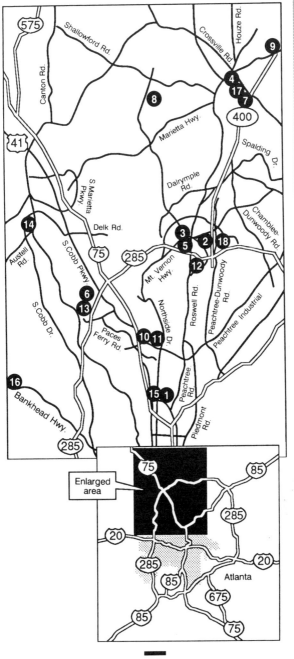

NORTHWEST

Dining at a Glance

Map	Fare	Attire	Cost
1 Bernard's	French	Dressy	$$$
2 Chequers Bar & Grill	American	Informal	$$$
3 Dai Nam Vietnamese Cuisine	Far East	Casual	$
4 El Mexica	Mexican	Informal	$$
5 Embers Seafood Grill	Seafood	Informal	$$$
6 Haveli	Indian	Informal	$$
7 La Grotta	Italian	Very dressy	$$$
8 La Strada	Italian	Informal	$$
9 Lickskillet Farm	American	Informal	$$$
10 OK Cafe	American	Informal	$$
11 Pano's & Paul's	Continental	Very dressy	$$$
12 Papa Pirozki's	Russian	Dressy	$$$
13 The Patio By The River	French	Dressy	$$$
14 The Planters	American	Dressy	$$$
15 U.S. Bar y Grill	Tex-Mex	Informal	$$
16 Wallace Barbecue	Southern	Casual	$
17 Waterstone's	Continental	Informal	$$$
18 Wickers	American	Dressy	$$$

KEY: $-full meal under $10; $$-from $10-$25; $$$-more than $25

❶ **Bernard's.** 1193 Collier Rd. N.W., 352-2778. French. Cozy bistro, favored by business people. Choice: rack of lamb. Dressy. $$$. Food/B. Comfort/B. Lunch weekdays and dinner Monday-Saturday. Major credit cards, reservations.

2 Chequers Bar & Grill. 236 Perimeter Center Parkway, Dunwoody, 391-9383. American. Fresh seafood, atmosphere of a business-hotel's dining room. Popular. Choice: mesquite-grilled fish. Informal. $$$. Food/C. Comfort/B. Lunch and dinner daily. Major credit cards, reservations, no-smoking section.

3 Dai Nam Vietnamese Cuisine. Lower level, Parkside Shopping Center, 5920 Roswell Rd., Sandy Springs, 256-2340. Vietnamese, and some of the town's best. Chef Kiet Changivy's cooking is heavily influenced by Paris and California. Specialties include charcoal-grilled Chinese eggplant and whole grilled fish with fresh herbs. Choice: rum raisin ice cream and filtered coffee with sweetened, condensed milk. Casual. $. Food/B. Comfort/D. Lunch and dinner Monday-Friday; late lunch through dinner on Saturdays and Sundays. Checks accepted but not credit cards. Smoky.

4 El Mexica. 408 South Atlanta St. (Clock Tower Place), Roswell, 594-8674. Mexican. Excellent south-of-border fare in a new location. Choice: Steak Taco Paco. Informal. $$. Food/B. Comfort/B. Lunch Monday-Saturday; dinner daily. Major credit cards, reservations.

5 Embers Seafood Grill. 234 Hilderbrand Dr. (at Roswell Rd.), Sandy Springs, 256-0977. Seafood. Grilled and blackened fish in a converted house. Local favorite. Choice: ask what's freshest. Informal. $$$. Food/B. Comfort/B. Dinner nightly. Major credit cards.

6 Haveli. 2706 Cobb Parkway, Smyrna, 955-4525. Indian. Stylish Indian restaurant specializing in tandoori (clay oven) cooking. Lunch buffet a bargain. Choice: tandoori chicken. Informal. $$. Food/B. Comfort/B. Lunch Monday-Saturday; dinner daily. Major credit cards.

7 La Grotta Ristorante Italiano. 647 N. Atlanta St., Roswell, 998-0645. Northern Italian. Branch of the Buckhead location.

8 La Strada. 2930 Johnson Ferry Rd. (near Lassiter Rd.), Marietta, 640-7008. Italian. Neo-realism comes to Cobb. Culinary and managerial ideas are derived from Buckhead's now-defunct, once-upscale Capriccio. Prices are low. Value high. Choice: squid steak, rigatoni with sausage and escarole, creme brulee. Informal. $$. Food/B. Comfort/C. Dinner nightly. Major credit cards; no reservations, not wheelchair friendly.

9 Lickskillet Farm. Old Roswell Rd. (at Rockmill Rd.), Roswell, 475-6484. American. Antebellum farmhouse offering complete dinners, Sunday brunch, in comfortably elegant surroundings. Choice: chicken livers. Informal. $$$. Food/ C. Comfort/B. Dinner Monday-Saturday. Major credit cards, reservations.

10 OK Cafe ●. 1284 W. Paces Ferry Rd. N.W. (at Northside Parkway), 262-3336. American. Cleverly decorated faux diner serving frisky food in fashionable neighborhood. Choice: grilled cheese sandwich, onion rings. Informal. $$. Food/ B. Comfort/B. Lunch and dinner daily. Sunday brunch. Major credit cards.

11 Pano's & Paul's ★ ●. 1232 W. Paces Ferry Rd. N.W., 261-3662. Continental. Gilded Age decor, luxury wining and dining for those who know (and can pay for) exactly what they want. Choice: desserts. Very dressy. $$$. Food/A. Comfort/A. Dinner nightly except Sundays. Major credit cards, reservations.

12 Papa Pirozki's. 4953 Roswell Rd., 252-1118. Russian. Cleverly decorated cafe with dramatic, inconsistent food and drink. Choice: pirozkis, flavored vodkas. Dressy. $$$. Food/C. Comfort/B. Lunch weekdays; dinner nightly except Sundays. Major credit cards, reservations, valet parking.

⓭ The Patio By The River. 4199 Paces Ferry Rd. N.W. (northwest bank of the Chattahoochee River), Vinings, 432-2808. French. Handsome old-brick building spiffed up with modern art, antique china, herb garden. Hangout for the well-heeled neighborhood. Superior wine list. Choice: mussel soup, lamb chops on the river-front terrace. Dressy. $$$. Food/B. Comfort/B. Lunch weekdays, dinner nightly except Sundays. Major credit cards, reservations.

⓮ The Planters. 789 South Cobb Dr., Marietta, 427-4646. American. Greek revival, 1848 mansion—a perfect stand-in for Ashley Wilkes' Twelve Oaks. Kitchen occasionally errs on the side of trendiness. Pleasant service, appointments and exceptional wine list take up the slack. Choice: seasonal menu. Dressy. $$$. Food/B. Comfort/A. Dinner Monday-Saturday. Lunch for groups by reservation. Major credit cards, valet parking, reservations requested.

⓯ U.S. Bar y Grill. 2002 Howell Mill Rd. (at Collier Rd.), 352-0033. Tex-Mex. Cantina atmosphere draws a young crowd for long-neck beer and mesquite-roasted cabrito (baby goat). Choice: cabrito al pastor. Informal. $$. Food/B. Comfort/ C. Major credit cards.

⓰ Wallace Barbecue. 3035 Bankhead Hwy, Austell, 739-1686. Southern. Pig out here if you're nearby. Pork ribs are tender, juicy, small but admirably lean. Chopped and sliced pork is smoky, agreeably sweet-sour and slightly dry. Service is informal, friendly, and faster than a greased pig sliding downhill. Choice: baked Idaho potato stuffed with American cheese and chopped barbecue pork. Casual. $. Food/B. Comfort/B. Lunch and dinner Tuesday-Saturday. Checks accepted, but no credit cards. No reservations at rush hours. No alcohol. Separate takeout area.

NORTHWEST ATLANTA DINING

17 **Waterstone's.** 555 S. Atlanta St., Roswell Mill, 594-8362. Continental. Eclectic, comfy menu and decor, excellent chef and wine service. Choice: duck, veal, lemon pie. Informal. $$. Food/B. Comfort/B. Dinner Tuesday-Saturday. Major credit cards, reservations.

18 **Wickers.** Hyatt Regency Ravinia, 4355 Ashford-Dunwoody Rd., Dunwoody, 395-1234. American. Dramatic woodland views by day, spot-lit kitchen at night in this luxurious hotel dining room. Choice: stir-fried wild mushroom salad. Dressy. $$$. Food/B. Comfort/A. Lunch daily except Saturdays; dinner daily except Sundays. Major credit cards, reservations.

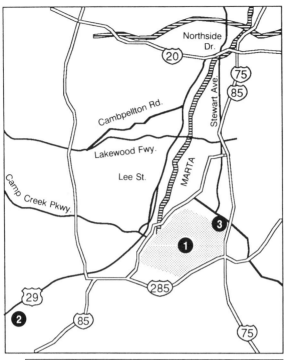

Northside Dr.

20

75

85

Cambpellton Rd.

Stewart Ave.

Lakewood Fwy.

Lee St.

MARTA

Camp Creek Pkwy.

3

1

29

2

285

85

75

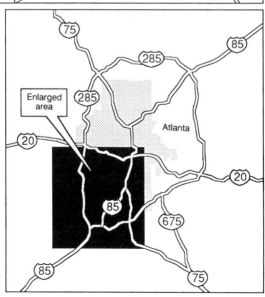

75

85

285

Enlarged area

285

Atlanta

20

20

85

675

85

75

SOUTH

Dining at a Glance

Map	Fare	Attire	Cost
1 Le Cygne	Continental	Dressy	$$$
2 Melear's	Southern	Casual	$
3 Zur Bratwurst Bavarian	German	Informal	$$

KEY: $-full meal under $10; $$-from $10-$25; $$$-more than $25

❶ Le Cygne. Ramada Renaissance Hotel, Atlanta Airport, 762-7676. Continental. Best fancy-dining bet near Hartsfield. Comfortable room, private. Choice: grilled fresh fish. Dressy. $$$. Food/B. Comfort/B. Lunch weekdays; dinner nightly except Sundays. Shuttle available from the airport baggage claim area. Major credit cards, reservations.

❷ Melear's. Highway 29, Union City, 964-9933. Southern. Pit-cooked barbecue beef and pork, the real stuff—some think the best. Choice: sliced pork barbecue. Casual. $. Food/B. Comfort/C. Open daily for breakfast, lunch and dinner. No major credit cards.

❸ Zur Bratwurst Bavarian Restaurant.

529 North Central Ave., Hapeville, 763-4068. German. Schnitzel, bratens, salats, kartoffel, wursts (five styles) und bier. Mit recorded oom-pa-pa-pop, yet. Service is motherly but swift. Choice: Oktoberfestwurst, mashed potatoes, kraut. Food/C. Comfort/C. Informal. $$. Lunch weekdays; dinner Monday-Saturday. Major credit cards, reservations. Restrooms not wheelchair friendly.

NIGHTLIFE

Willie Nelson notwithstanding, the nightlife *is* the good life in Atlanta. From the vibrant nightspots of Kenny's Alley in Underground to the glitz of the Buckhead clubs, you can find the place to suit your taste.

NIGHTLIFE

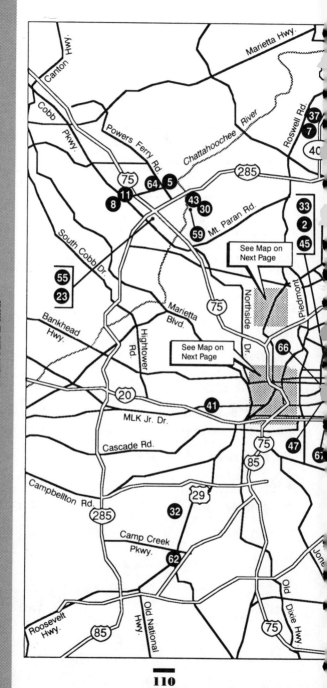

See Map on Next Page

See Map on Next Page

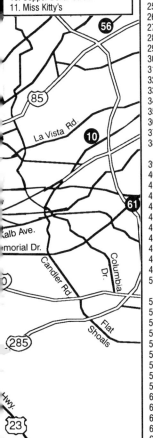

1. Blues Harbor
2. Blind Willie's
3. Royal Peacock
4. Comedy Act Theatre
5. A Comic Cafe
6. Funny Bone Comedy Club of Buckhead
7. The Punch Line, Sandy Springs
8. Buckhead Country Showcase
9. Carey's Buckhead Longbranch
10. Copper Dollar Saloon
11. Miss Kitty's
12. Miss Kitty's Saloon & Dance Hall
13. The Cafe Bar
14. Candide
15. Club 112
16. Club Anytime
17. Club D
18. Johnny's Hideaway
19. Petrus
20. Rupert's
21. Savoy Restaurant and Lounge
22. Studebaker's
23. Stouffer Waverly Hotel
24. V's on Peachtree
25. Weekends and Tunnelvision
26. The Bistro
27. The Lobby Lounge
28. The Ritz-Carlton, Atlanta
29. Churchill Arms Pub
30. Coffee House
31. County Cork Pub
32. Joyful Noise
33. Limerick Junction
34. Rio Bravo Cantina
35. A-Train
36. The Bar
37. Cafe 290
38. Dante's Down the Hatch Jazz Night Club
39. Otto's
40. The Parrot
41. Paschal's La Carousel Lounge
42. Public House
43. Ray's on the River
44. Sounds of Buckhead
45. Atkins Park
46. Jocks and Jills
47. Manuel's Tavern
48. O'Henry's
49. Country Place
50. McKinnon's Louisiane Restaurant and Seafood Grill
51. Park Place Cafe
52. Peachtree Cafe
53. Peasant Uptown
54. Dailey's
55. Winfield's
56. The Wooden Nickel Pub
57. The Cavern
58. Chameleon Club
59. Charlie Magruder's
60. Cotton Club
61. Player's Retreat
62. R & R Nite Club
63. Another World
64. Club 21
65. Good Ol' Days, Buckhead
66. The Masquerade
67. The Point
68. Spring Break

NIGHTLIFE MAP

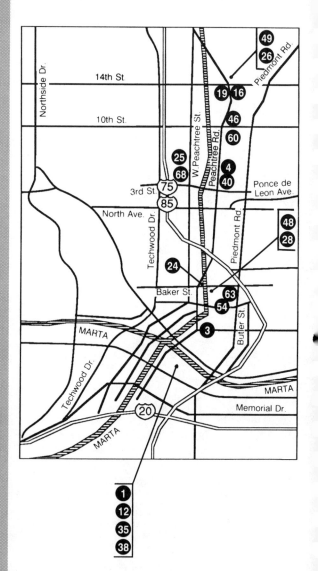

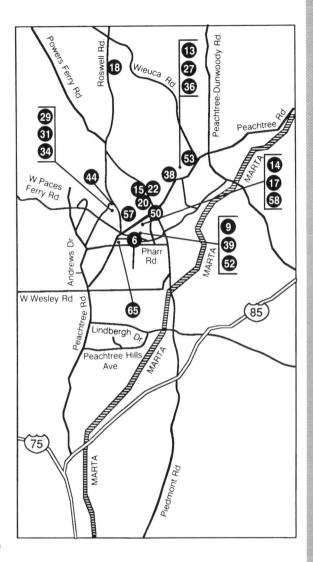

BLUES

1 **Blues Harbor.** Underground Atlanta, 524-3001. See **Underground** section.

2 **Blind Willie's.** 828 North Highland N.E., 873-2583. The music is raw and the decor is Early Smoky Dive. There's a neon alligator to greet you in the window of this cramped Virginia-Highland storefront. Opens at 6 p.m. with music from 10 p.m.-2 a.m. nightly. Mixed drinks. Major credit cards. Casual. Serves food. Cover charge varies.

3 **Royal Peacock.** 186½ Auburn Ave. N.E., 880-0745. This was Atlanta's Apollo Theatre in the '50s and '60s, where Little Richard often belted out his best. Rhythm & Blues and Blues are the specialty of the house now. Open Friday-Sunday nights. Mixed drinks. Major credit cards. Casual to party attire. Call for entertainment schedule and cost of shows.

COMEDY

4 **Comedy Act Theatre.** 917 Peachtree St. at Eighth St., 875-3550. A unique showcase for established and amateur comedic performers, featuring black stand-up comedians. Doors open at 8 p.m. Shows at 8:30 p.m. Tuesday-Saturday; additional performances at 11:45 p.m. Friday and

Saturday. Mixed drinks. Casual. Cover charge: $6
Tuesday-Thursday; $10 Friday and Saturday.

❺ A Comic Cafe. 1215 Powers Ferry Rd., Marietta (Powers Ferry Plaza Shopping Center, Delk
Rd. at Powers Ferry), 956-7827. A local stop on
the national comedy circuit. Opens at 7 p.m.
Shows at 8:30 p.m. Tuesday-Saturday; second
show on Friday and Saturday at 10 p.m. Closed
Sunday and Monday. Mixed drinks. Major credit
cards. Casual. Serves food. Cover charge varies
with act.

❻ Funny Bone Comedy Club of Buckhead.
247 Buckhead Ave., 266-3555. Features local and
national acts. Shows begin at 8:30 p.m. Tuesday-
Sunday; additional show on Friday and Saturday
at 10:45 p.m. Mixed drinks. Major credit cards.
Casual. Serves food. Cover charge: $6 and $7
weekdays; $10 and $11 weekends (higher prices
are for reserved seats).

❼ The Punch Line, Sandy Springs.
Balconies Shopping Center, 280 Hilderbrand Dr.
(off Roswell Rd., half-mile north of I-285),
252-5233. This, the original Punch Line, spawned
a national chain of comedy clubs. Three performances nightly. Shows at 8:30 p.m. Tuesday-
Thursday; 8:30 p.m. and 10:45 p.m. Friday; 7:30
p.m., 9:45 p.m., and 11:45 p.m. Saturday; and
8:30 p.m. Sunday. Mixed drinks. Major credit
cards. Casual. Serves food. Call for reservations
and prices.

COUNTRY

❽ Buckboard Country Music Showcase.
2080 Cobb Parkway (in Windy Hill Plaza),
Smyrna, 955-7340. Down-home, blue-collar
country-and-western, featuring a local band
nightly and national acts on a weekly basis. Opens
at 11 a.m. weekdays and 6 p.m. on Saturdays.
Closed on Sunday. Music from 9 p.m.-2 a.m.
Monday-Friday; 9 p.m.-2:55 a.m., Saturday. Mixed

drinks. Major credit cards. Casual. Serves food. Cover charge: $3, weekdays; $5, Friday and Saturday. Cover charge varies on national showcases.

9 Carey's Buckhead Longbranch. 288 E. Paces Ferry Rd., 239-9650. This fun country-western bar is located in the heart of Buckhead. In addition to the country-western music, a reggae band entertains outside during the summer. Open: 11 a.m.-1 a.m. daily, but hours extended until 4 a.m. on the weekends. Music on Friday and Saturday nights only, beginning at 9 p.m. In the summer months, music may be heard six nights a week. Mixed drinks. Major credit cards. Casual. Serves food. Cover charge on weekends is $2.

10 Copper Dollar Saloon. 2272 Lawrenceville Hwy., Decatur, 325-5342. Rock out with the tunes of the country-rock group, Big Dollar Band. Pool and darts, too, attract visitors to this popular watering hole. Open 11:30 a.m.-4 a.m. Monday-Friday and 12:30 p.m.-3 a.m. Saturday and Sunday. Music starts at 9:30 p.m. Wednesday-Sunday. Mixed drinks. Major credit cards. Casual. Serves food. Cover charge: $3 Tuesday-Saturday except Thursday which is Ladies' Night (ladies get in free and drink at half-price).

11 Miss Kitty's. 1038 Franklin Rd., Marietta, 424-6556. Do the two-step, polka, and western swing to the sounds of country-rock bands. Free dance lessons Monday and Tuesday. The club sometimes offers national acts. Shows at 9 p.m. Monday-Saturday. Mixed drinks. Major credit cards. Casual. Serves food. Cover charge: $3 on weekends, free on weekdays.

12 Miss Kitty's Saloon & Dance Hall. Underground, 524-4614. See **UNDERGROUND**.

DANCING

⓭ The Cafe Bar. The Ritz-Carlton, Buckhead, 3434 Peachtree Rd. N.E., 237-2700. A pleasant place to enjoy easy listening and popular dance music. On Fridays it becomes a ballroom of yesteryear with tea dances accompanied by The William Noll Quartet. Open 5 p.m.-midnight Monday-Thursday and 5 p.m.-1 a.m. Friday and Saturday. Live music on the weekends starting around 8 p.m. Tea dances 5-8 p.m. on Friday. Mixed drinks. Major credit cards. Casual attire admitted, but coat and tie preferred. Serves food. No cover charge.

⓮ Candide. 3055 Peachtree St. N.E., 231-1574. Known as a disco with current progressive club mixes, Candide is comprised of three rooms: the main lounge with its aquarium and cushy furniture, the art gallery, and the dance room with its fluorescent wall murals. Open 9 p.m.-4 a.m. Wednesday-Friday; 9 p.m.-3 a.m. Saturday. Mixed drinks. Major credit cards. Casual, but no tennis shoes. Cover charge: $3 Wednesday and Thursday; $7 on weekends.

⓯ Club 112. 3330 Piedmont Rd., 261-0155. For the energized folks who just keep going and going.... You could truly dance all night here to the tunes of the latest music and breakfast on eggs or omelets when you are sitting one out. Open 12 a.m.-7 a.m. daily. Mixed drinks. Major credit cards. Casual. Serves food. Cover charge varies; call for information.

16 Club Anytime. 1055 Peachtree St., 607-8050. High energy dance music is the fare at this Midtown club with its arty decor. Open seven days a week, around the clock. Bands start playing at 11 p.m. For night owls, deejays spin records into the wee hours of the morning. Mixed drinks. Major credit cards. Neat, but casual attire. Serves food. Cover charge: generally $5 on weekdays and $8 on weekends.

17 Club D. 3063 Peachtree St. N.E., 240-0429. A piano bar featuring contemporary music and a dance club with high energy dance music are the dual attractions at this Buckhead hot spot. Open 8 p.m.-3 a.m. Tuesday-Sunday. Music starts at 9 p.m. Mixed drinks. Major credit cards. Party attire. Cover charge: $3 Friday and Saturday nights only.

18 Johnny's Hideaway. 3771 Roswell Rd., 233-8026. Dance to Beach Music here on Sunday, Monday and Wednesday, and even take a free lesson in the Shag on Monday. A different beat is heard on Tuesday and Thursday-Saturday when the Big Band sound beckons its fans. Open 11 a.m.-4 a.m. Monday-Friday; noon-3 a.m. Saturday; noon-4 a.m. Sunday. Music starts at 9 p.m. Mixed drinks. Major credit cards. Nice casual attire. Serves food, including a free spaghetti dinner on Sunday night at 5 p.m. No cover charge.

19 Petrus. 1150 Peachtree St. N.E., 873-6700. High-powered dance music in this glitzy disco. Live music occasionally, but the discs spin most nights. Open for dancing at 8 p.m. Tuesday-Friday and Sunday; 9 p.m. on Saturday. Wednesday is Ladies' Night. Mixed drinks. Major credit cards. Casual. Food in the video bar/cafe. Cover charge: $3 Sunday and Tuesday; $5 Wednesday-Friday; $7 Saturday.

20 Rupert's. 3330 Piedmont Rd. N.E. (Peachtree-Piedmont Crossing Shopping Center), 266-9834. High-energy dance music from a sizzling 16-piece orchestra in a sophisticated, elegant atmosphere. Open 5:30 p.m.-2 a.m. Tuesday-Thursday; 5:30 p.m.-3 a.m. Friday; 8 p.m.-3 a.m. Saturday; closed Sunday and Monday. Mixed drinks. Major credit cards. Party attire. Serves food. Cover charge: $4 after 8 p.m. weekdays; $7 after 8 p.m. weekends.

21 Savoy Restaurant and Lounge. 2117 Savoy Dr., Chamblee, 451-1515. Organist Bob Fountain plays '30s and '40s music for dancing and sing-along. Open 11 a.m. Entertainment schedule: 8 p.m.-1 a.m. Tuesday-Thursday; 8 p.m.-3 a.m. Friday and Saturday; 7 p.m.-11 p.m. Sunday. Mixed drinks. Major credit cards. Dressy. Serves food. No cover charge.

22 Studebaker's. The Courtyard at Tower Place, 3365 Piedmont Rd., 266-9856. Since 1980, baby boomers have been dancing in this classic malt-shop setting in Buckhead. Music from the '50s to the '80s. Learn to dance the Shag every Tuesday. Ladies' Night (with free admission for women) is every Thursday. Opens at 5 p.m. Monday-Friday; at 8 p.m. Saturday. Mixed drinks. Major credit cards. Casual. Serves food. Cover charge varies according to time and night.

23 Stouffer Waverly Hotel. 2450 Galleria Parkway N.W., 953-4500. The Don Miolla Orchestra plays music of the Big Band era in the hotel's atrium lobby. Live music at 7 p.m. on Friday. Mixed drinks. Major credit cards. Cocktail attire. Serves food. Cover charge: $10 per person.

24 V's on Peachtree. 320 Peachtree St. N.E., 522-3021. Deejays spin R & B, soul, and Top 40 tunes for the dancing crowd. Open 5 p.m.-4 a.m. Tuesday-Thursday; 4 p.m.-4 a.m. Friday; and 8 p.m.-3 a.m. Saturday. Music starts when the doors open. Ladies' night is Thursday. Mixed drinks. Major credit cards. Cosmopolitan. Serves food on

DANCING

Wednesday-Friday only (buffet). Cover charge: $6 after 9 p.m. Thursday-Saturday.

㉕ Weekends and **Tunnelvision.** 688 Spring St., 875-5835. Recorded progressive dance music with live entertainment on weekends at Tunnelvision. Weekends imposes a 21-year-old age limit, but Tunnelvision admits those 18 and older. Open 10 p.m.-4 a.m. Wednesday-Sunday (except 3 a.m. closing on Saturday). Music starts at 10 p.m. Mixed drinks. Major credit cards. Casual. Serves food. Cover charge: $5.

EASY LISTENING

26 The Bistro. Colony Square Hotel, 188 14th
St. N.E., 892-6000. An open, airy lounge over-
looking the Midtown shopping mall. Monica plays
folk music on the weekends. Jazz is the fare on
weekdays. Opens at 6:30 p.m. daily. Music starts
at 9 p.m. and runs until midnight Tuesday-
Saturday. Mixed drinks. Major credit cards.
Casual. Serves food. No cover charge.

27 The Lobby Lounge. The Ritz-Carlton,
Buckhead, 3434 Peachtree Rd. N.E., 237-2700.
High tea is served weekdays while William Noll
plays classics on a Steinway concert piano. A
combo plays popular dance music in the early
evening. High tea from 3-5 p.m. and live music
5:30-8 p.m., 365 days a year. Mixed drinks. Major
credit cards. Coat and tie preferred dress. Serves
food. No cover charge.

28 The Ritz-Carlton, Atlanta. 181 Peachtree
St. N.E., 659-0400. Tea is served in The Lobby
Lounge with a solo pianist playing primarily clas-
sical background music from 11:30 a.m.-5:30 p.m.,
daily. The Bar with its late-nineteenth-century
paintings and elegant decor features solo jazz
piano in the early evening and the Jerry Lambert
Trio playing contemporary and jazz music later.
Live music in The Bar from 6 p.m.-1 a.m. daily.
Mixed drinks. Major credit cards. Coat and tie.
Serves food. No cover charge.

FOLK, ETHNIC AND GOSPEL

㉙ Churchill Arms Pub. 3223 Cains Hill Place, 233-5633. Anglophile heaven in Buckhead. This British pub has darts, a commanding portrait of Sir Winston, and a sing-along piano player on weekends. Open 4 p.m. Monday-Saturday and 5 p.m. Sunday. Live music from 9 p.m. on Friday and Saturday. Mixed drinks. Major credit cards. Casual. Serves food. No cover charge.

㉚ Coffee House. Unitarian Congregation, 1025 Mount Vernon Hwy., Sandy Springs, 955-1408. Amateur folk music is performed the first Friday of each month. Solo and group performances. Music from 8 p.m.-11 p.m. Beer and wine are the only alcohol served. Cash only. Casual. Serves snacks. $3 donation requested.

㉛ County Cork Pub. Ste. 16, 56 E. Andrews Dr. N.W., 262-2227. This Irish pub has darts and authentic live music. Opens at 3 p.m. and music begins at 8:30 p.m. Tuesday and Wednesday; 9 p.m. Thursday-Saturday. Mixed drinks. Major credit cards. Casual. Serves food. Cover charge: $1 Thursday-Saturday.

㉜ Joyful Noise. 2669 Church St., East Point, 768-5100. A Christian supper club with nationally known gospel music. Open Thursday-Sunday. Call for reservations and schedule. No alcohol or smoking allowed. Major credit cards. Casual to dressy. Serves food. Prices vary according to performance.

㉝ Limerick Junction. 822 N. Highland Ave., 874-7147. Features Irish folk music and a rip-roaring good time on St. Patrick's Day. Live entertainment nightly features a soloist or duo. Sunday night is jazz night; Monday is ballad night; Tuesday night is "Open mike" or amateur night with a cash prize awarded; Wednesday-Saturday nights feature traditional Irish music. Hours: 5 p.m.-midnight Sunday; 5 p.m.-1 a.m. Monday-

Wednesday; 5 p.m.-2 a.m. Thursday-Saturday. Music starts at 9 p.m. "Open mike" begins at 8 p.m. Mixed drinks. Major credit cards. Casual. Serves Food. Cover charge: $1 Friday and Saturday only.

34 **Rio Bravo Cantina.** 3172 Roswell Rd. N.W., 262-7431. Primarily a Mexican restaurant, this is also a popular Buckhead gathering spot for locals who enjoy Mexican beer and frozen margaritas to the accompaniment of a strolling mariachi band. Open 11:30 a.m.; band plays 7-11:30 p.m. Tuesday-Saturday. Mixed drinks. Major credit cards. Casual. No cover charge.

JAZZ

35 **A-Train.** See **Underground** section.

36 **The Bar.** The Ritz-Carlton, Buckhead, 3434 Peachtree St. N.E., 237-2700. In this elegant club room reminiscent of New York's Carlyle, you can experience a variety of jazz. The Gary Motley Trio is a cool jazz ensemble which performs from 8 p.m.-midnight on Thursday and from 8 p.m.-1 a.m. on Friday and Saturday. Special guest stars often join the group on weekends. Zoltan Csanyi plays easy-listening music Monday-Wednesday nights starting at 8 p.m. Day people can drop in on Cynthia Davis for some easy listening from noon-2:30 p.m. any weekday or hear Bill Davis play jazz from 4:30 p.m.-8 p.m. Monday-Saturday. Mixed drinks. Major credit cards. Casual attire is admitted, but coat and tie preferred. Serves food. No cover charge.

37 **Cafe 290.** 290 Hilderbrand Ave., 256-3942. This restaurant/bar showcases good local jazz bands in a relaxed and casual neighborhood atmosphere. In addition to the music, Cafe 290 also operates a sports bar which opens at noon on weekends. Opens at 5 p.m. Monday-Friday and at noon on Saturday and Sunday. Live music from 8:30 p.m.-1:30 a.m. Sunday-Thursday; 8:30

p.m.-2:30 a.m. Friday and Saturday. Mixed
drinks. Major credit cards. Casual. Serves food.
No cover charge.

38 Dante's Down the Hatch Jazz Nightclub.
3380 Peachtree St. N.E. (across from Lenox
Square), 266-1600. Long a fixture of Underground
Atlanta, this location opened when the old Underground Atlanta closed, but both Buckhead and
the new Underground are privileged to have their
own Dante's now. A replica of an eighteenth-
century sailing ship surrounded by a Mediterranean fishing village consumes the space in the restaurant and bar — with live crocodiles in the moat.
The Paul Mitchell Trio plays soft jazz on a regular basis aboard the ship. A classical guitarist
plays on the wharf. Music schedule: guitarist plays
6 p.m.-midnight Monday; guitarist plays 6-8 p.m.
and The Paul Mitchell Trio plays 8 p.m.-midnight
Tuesday-Thursday; jazz pianist performs 6:30-8
p.m. and The Paul Mitchell Trio performs 8
p.m.-1 a.m. Friday and Saturday. On Sunday evening The Paul Mitchell Trio is on from 7-11 p.m.
Mixed drinks. Major credit cards. Casual to party
attire. Serves food. Cover charge: no fee on the
wharf; $4 per person is added to the check for
seating on the ship.

39 Otto's. 265 E. Paces Ferry Rd. N.E.,
233-1133. This New York-style club with jazz
music by Tony Winston is a favorite of baby
boomers and yuppies. Open 5:30 p.m.-2 a.m.
Monday-Thursday and until at least 3 a.m. on
weekends. Music starts at 9:30 p.m. Mixed drinks.
Major credit cards. Informal. No cover charge.

40 The Parrot. 571 Peachtree St., 873-3165.
Enjoy the soft touch of jazz with Gloria Sessom
on Tuesday and Wednesday or meld with the tones
of the William Green Band Thursday-Sunday in
this New York-style cabaret. Opens 5 p.m.
Tuesday-Thursday; 4 p.m. Friday; 9 p.m. Saturday and 8 p.m. Sunday. Music starts at 9 p.m.
except on Saturday when it begins at 10 p.m.
Mixed drinks. Major credit cards. Informal. Cover
charge: $6 Friday and Saturday only.

41 Paschal's La Carousel Lounge. 830 Martin Luther King, Jr., Dr. S.W., 577-3150. Jazz and urban contemporary music for dancing are provided by nationally famous jazz artists at this vintage jazz club in southwest Atlanta. Open 2 p.m.-2 a.m. Monday-Saturday. Music nightly from 9 p.m.-2 a.m. Mixed drinks. Major credit cards. Party attire. Serves light food. No cover charge.

42 Public House. Roswell Square, 605 Atlanta St., Roswell, 992-4646. Benjy Templeton plays contemporary jazz. Opens 5:30 p.m. Music from 6-10 p.m. Wednesday and Thursday; 7 p.m.-midnight Friday and Saturday. No music on Sunday-Tuesday. Mixed drinks. Major credit cards. Casual. Serves food. No cover charge.

43 Ray's on the River. 6700 Powers Ferry Rd., 955-1187. 6700 Powers Ferry Rd., 955-1187. Discover the joys of contemporary jazz in the music of Elgin Wells at this picturesque spot on the Chattahoochee River. Music from 8 p.m.-midnight Monday-Thursday; 9 p.m.-1 a.m. Friday and Saturday. Mixed drinks. Major credit cards. Casual. Serves food. No cover charge.

44 Sounds of Buckhead. 128 E. Andrews Dr., 262-1377. Revisit the heyday of the supper club with an evening at this favorite nightspot. Live jazz for listening and dancing can be heard starting at 8 p.m. The restaurant and lounge are open 6 p.m.-11:30 p.m. Tuesday-Thursday; 6 p.m.-3 a.m. Friday and Saturday. In addition to the American dinner fare, late night breakfast is also served. Mixed drinks. Major credit cards. Informal or party attire. Cover charge: two drink minimum in cocktail lounge.

JAZZ

NEIGHBORHOOD BARS

45 Atkins Park. 794 North Highland Ave., 876-7249. Located in one of the city's oldest neighborhoods, this restaurant/tavern has been popular with locals since the '20s. Open 11 a.m.-4 a.m. Monday-Friday; 10:30 a.m.-3 a.m. Saturday and 10:30 a.m.-4 a.m. Sunday. Mixed drinks. Major credit cards. Casual. Serves food. Serves brunch on Saturday and Sunday.

46 Jocks and Jills. 112 10th St. N.E., 873-5405. A sports bar/restaurant with two satellite dishes, 19 television sets, and plenty of sports memorabilia. Open 11:30 a.m. daily. Mixed drinks. Major credit cards. Casual. Serves food.

47 Manuel's Tavern. 602 North Highland Ave., 525-3447. This neighborhood bar has been an institution in Atlanta since 1956. The owner, a colorful character named Manuel Maloof, may often be seen serving a brew to local politicians and media types who haunt the bar. Open 10:30 a.m.-2 a.m. Monday-Saturday; noon-11 p.m. Sunday. Mixed drinks. Major credit cards. Casual. Serves food.

48 O'Henry's. 230 Peachtree St. in Peachtree Center, 524-5175. Captures the friendliness and camaraderie of a neighborhood tavern despite its location in a skyscraper canyon and the predominance of business suits and conventioneers. Open 11:30 a.m.-10 p.m. Monday-Friday; 5:30 p.m.-10 p.m. Saturday and Sunday.

PIANO BARS

49 Country Place. Colony Square Hotel, Peachtree at 14th Sts., 881-0144. Gershwin and Porter and light classics on piano. Open 11 a.m. daily except Saturday when opening time is 5 p.m. Music from 7-11 p.m. Mixed drinks. Major credit cards. Casual to dressy. Serves food.

50 McKinnon's Louisiane Restaurant and Seafood Grill. 3209 Maple Dr. at Peachtree Rd., 237-1313. Although best known as a Cajun restaurant, patrons at this Buckhead spot enjoy the performance piano bar where you can just listen or join in a sing-along. Fran Irwin is on the piano from 7 p.m.-midnight Tuesday-Saturday. Mixed drinks. Major credit cards. Casual to dressy. Serves food. No cover charge.

51 Park Place Cafe. 4505 Ashford-Dunwoody Rd. (Park Place Shopping Center), 399-5990. A small, elegant piano bar with funky pop music where northside business people loosen up. Open 11:30 a.m.-2 a.m. Monday-Thursday; 11:30 a.m.-4 a.m. Friday; 6 p.m.-3 a.m. Saturday. Mixed drinks. Major credit cards. Casual. Serves food. No cover charge.

52 Peachtree Cafe. 268 E. Paces Ferry Rd., 233-4402. Listen to the sounds of pop or jazz with Alan Callais at the piano at this trendy Buckhead spot. Opens daily at 11 a.m. Music starts at 9 p.m. Wednesday-Saturday. Mixed drinks. Major credit cards. Casual. Serves food. No cover charge.

53 Peasant Uptown. 3500 Peachtree Rd. N.E. (Phipps Plaza), 261-6341. A solo pianist plays show tunes and standards in the lounge adjacent to the restaurant. Open 11 a.m. daily. Music 7 p.m.-closing nightly. Mixed drinks. Major credit cards. Casual to dressy. Serves food. No cover charge.

PIANO BARS

127

POP

54 Dailey's. 17 International Blvd. N.E., 681-3303. This downtown restaurant, located in a former warehouse, features live jazz and pop nightly. Late-night desserts are a specialty. Open at 11 a.m. Music from 8 p.m.-11 p.m. Tuesday-Saturday. Mixed drinks. Major credit cards. Casual. Serves food. No cover charge.

55 Winfield's. Galleria Specialty Mall, 100 Galleria Pkwy., 955-5300. Pop and jazz on piano. Open 11:30 a.m. Music 7-11 p.m. Tuesday-Saturday. Mixed drinks. Major credit cards. Casual. Serves food. No cover charge.

56 The Wooden Nickel Pub. 3201 Tucker Norcross Rd., Tucker, 939-5110. A relaxed neighborhood pub featuring the group Modern Men brings the Top 40 to life for your listening and dancing enjoyment. Opens at 11:30 a.m. Monday-Saturday and at 2:30 p.m. Sunday. Music from 8 p.m.-1 a.m. Wednesday-Saturday. Mixed drinks. Major credit cards. Casual. Serves food. No cover charge.

ROCK

57 The Cavern. 3227 Roswell Rd., 233-5903. The live rock bands here run the gamut from progressive and alternative rock 'n' roll to heavy metal. Open every day but Tuesday. Doors open at 9 p.m. Music starts at 10:30 p.m. Mixed drinks. Major credit cards. Casual. Serves food. Cover charge varies according to act, but usually ranges between $3 and $5.

58 Chameleon Club. 3179 Peachtree Rd. N.E., 261-8004. This Buckhead club showcases live entertainment with a progressive rock bent by regional talent. Open 9 p.m.-4 a.m. Wednesdayunday (except Saturday closing is at 3 a.m.). Sundays are Discomania nights when the club turns into a mock '70s disco. Mixed drinks. Major credit cards. Casual. Serves food. Cover charge varies according to act and night (never exceeds $7).

59 Charlie Magruder's. 6300 Powers Ferry Rd. N.W., 955-1157. A jumping night spot with live rock groups several nights each week. Open 7:30 p.m.-4 a.m. Monday-Friday; 7:30 p.m.-3 a.m. Saturday; and 10 p.m.-4 a.m. Sunday. Music starts at 11 p.m. Monday-Friday; 10:30 p.m. Saturday; 11:30 p.m., Sunday. Mixed drinks. Major credit cards. Casual. Serves food. Cover charge: $2 Monday-Wednesday; $3 Thursday and Sunday; $6 Friday and Saturday.

60 Cotton Club. 1021 Peachtree St. N.E., 874-2523. Rock out to the sounds of local and national acts at the Cotton Club. Most of the featured bands have signed a major label deal and are on their first road tour, so you might get in on a group that will make it "big time" in the not too distant future. Mixed drinks. Major credit cards accepted at bar, but admission by cash only. Casual. Call for schedule, reservations, and prices.

61 Player's Retreat. 5471 Memorial Dr. (Memorial Square Shopping Center), Stone Mountain, 297-0600. For a different night out, dance to Top 40 records or opt for pool (league play Monday-Wednesday). Open 4 p.m.-2 a.m. Monday-Thursday; 4 p.m.-4 a.m. Friday; 1 p.m.-3 a.m. Saturday; and 1 p.m.-2 a.m. Sunday. Mixed drinks. Major credit cards. Casual. Serves food. Cover charge: $5 for 21 and older; $6 if younger than 21.

62 R & R Nite Club. Ramada Renaissance, 4736 Best Rd., College Park, 762-7676. A disc jockey spins Top 40 on Tuesday night, but Wednesday-Saturday the Torch Band plays live music. Opens at 4:30 p.m., Tuesday-Friday with a Happy Hour Buffet. Opens at 8 p.m. Saturday. During the week the music starts at 8:30 p.m., but begins at 9 p.m. on the weekend. Mixed drinks. Major credit cards. Casual to party attire. Serves food. Cover charge: $5 on weekends only.

VARIETY

63 Another World. Atlanta Hilton and Towers, 255 Courtland St. N.E. (Courtland and Harris Sts.), 659-2000. Located at the top of the downtown Hilton, this lounge offers recorded music from the '50s to current Top 40 and a nice view of the city skyline. Sometimes comedy acts are scheduled in lieu of the music. Open 6 p.m. Live music or comedy from 9:30 p.m.-1:30 a.m. Tuesday-Saturday. Mixed drinks. Major credit cards. Casual. Serves food. No cover charge.

64 Club 21. 3000 Windy Hill Rd., Marietta, 952-9333. Variety is definitely the operative word in this swinging night spot. A deejay plays everything from Top 40 to R&B for the dance crowd. Open 5 p.m.-2 a.m. Wednesday-Thursday; 5 p.m.-4 a.m. Friday and 8 p.m.-3 a.m. Saturday. Mixed drinks. Major credit cards. Party attire. Serves food. Cover charge: $7 after 8 p.m.; Thursday night is Ladies' Night.

65 Good Ol' Days, Buckhead. 3013 Peachtree Rd. N.E., 266-2597. Neighborhood bar/restaurant with outdoor patios where local acoustic musicians play, nightly. Open 11 a.m. Music 8 p.m.-midnight Sunday-Thursday; 9 p.m.-1 a.m. Friday and Saturday. Mixed drinks. Major credit cards. Casual. Serves food. Cover charge: $2 Friday and Saturday night only for bands in back room. Another location is at 5841 Roswell Rd., 257-9183.

66 The Masquerade. 695 North Ave. N.E., 577-8178. A variety of entertainment awaits you in the historic Excelsior Mill which consists of three clubs: Heaven, Hell, and Purgatory. Heaven provides alternative dance music, while Hell showcases national and regional talent as varied in style as the Village People and the Outlaws in its concert hall; Purgatory provides an arena for local talent, with Open Mike Night every Thursday. Open 9 p.m.-4 a.m. Wednesday-Sunday (except closing hour is 3 a.m. on Saturday). Music starts around 9 p.m. Mixed drinks. Major credit cards. Cosmopolitan. Serves food. Cover charge varies with event.

67 The Point. 420 Moreland Ave. N.E., 577-6468. Eclectic shows in Little Five Points play to an eclectic crowd. Doors open at 9 p.m. weekdays and 1 p.m. Saturday and Sunday. Music from 10:30 p.m.-1:30 a.m.. Mixed drinks. Major credit cards. Casual. Serves food. Cover charge: $3-$6, depending on night of the week and the act.

68 Spring Break 60 5th St. N.W., 874-3476. A variety of music from reggae to jazz to blues and rock. Wednesday is dance night. Open 8 p.m.-2 a.m. daily. Music starts at 9:30 p.m. Mixed drinks. Cash only. Casual. Serves food on some days. Cover charge at times.

SHOPPING

Once centralized in the downtown area, shopping in Atlanta (as in every other city) has burgeoned in the suburbs with the emergence of the mall. Still, there are neighborhoods in Atlanta which continue to support viable shopping areas where unusual merchandise can be found. Although no attempt is made in this section to ferret out locales beyond the perimeter, there are plenty of interesting and noteworthy shops beyond the boundaries of I-285. Historic Roswell, for instance, is a great spot for antique lovers.

A buying center for the gift and apparel trades, Atlanta hosts major shows at the downtown Merchandise and Apparel Marts on a regular basis. Stores in the Atlanta area reflect this connection and cater to a wide range of tastes and interests.

SHOPPING MALLS

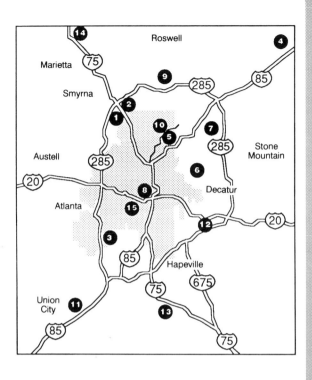

Shopping at a Glance

Map	Location
1 Cumberland Mall	Northwest: I-285 and U.S. 41
2 Galleria	Northwest: I-285 and U.S. 41
3 Greenbriar	South: Off I-285 and Lakewood Fwy.
4 Gwinnett Place	Northeast: I-85 and Pleasant Hill Rd.
5 Lenox Square	Buckhead: 3393 Peachtree Rd.
6 Market Square	Northeast: 2050 Lawrenceville Highway
7 Northlake Mall	Northeast: Off LaVista Rd. and I-285
8 Peachtree Center	Downtown: 224 Peachtree St.
9 Perimeter	North: 4400 Ashford-Dunwoody Rd.
10 Phipps Plaza	Buckhead: 3500 Peachtree Rd.
11 Shannon	South: Exit 13 off I-85 South
12 South DeKalb	East: Off I-20 at Candler Rd.
13 Southlake	South: Off I-75 South at Morrow exit
14 Town Center	Northwest: I-75 North to Barrett Pkwy.
15 West End Mall	S.W. Atlanta: 850 Oak St., S.W.

MALLS

A number of major enclosed shopping malls are located in metro Atlanta, each anchored by one or more department stores such as Rich's, Macy's, JC Penney, Mervyn's or Sears. Most are open 10 a.m.-9 p.m., Monday-Saturday and noon-6 p.m., Sunday. Many of them are within walking distance of MARTA bus or rail stops.

❶ Cumberland Mall. I-285 and U.S. 41. Cumberland Mall, with its anchors Sears, Rich's, JC Penney and Macy's is a mecca for folks from northwest Fulton and Cobb counties. Its 150 stores provide a large array of items for inveterate shoppers.

❷ Galleria. Across from Cumberland Mall at I-285 and U.S. 41 is The Galleria with its specialty shops and boutiques. A shopping corridor connects the mall to the lobby of the Waverly Hotel.

❸ Greenbriar. Located off I-285 and the Lakewood Freeway at 2841 Greenbriar Parkway, this mall serves the south Atlanta market and is anchored by Circuit City, Rich's and Upton's. Stores include a variety of national chains in the popular to moderate prices, a number of small food-service establishments and the regional Piccadilly Cafeteria.

4 Gwinnett Place. This mall has been open since 1984 at I-85 and Pleasant Hill Rd. with Macy's, Mervyn's, Rich's and Sears as its major stores. Gwinnett Place is easily accessible to Norcross, Lawrenceville, Lilburn, Snellville and points east and northeast of the city.

5 Lenox Square. Atlanta's first regional mall, Lenox Square opened in 1959 at 2293 Peachtree Rd., the site of an old country estate in Buckhead. The city's only Neiman Marcus store is here, along with Rich's and Macy's. The mall has undergone many lives, the latest of which connects it to the Westin Lenox Hotel at Lenox and East Paces Ferry roads. Designers Laura Ashley, Alexander Julian and Ralph Lauren all have branch locations here along with Louis Vuitton, Ann Taylor and Carroll Reed of New England. Sharper Image, Disney Store, Nature Company and Banana Republic delight catalog fans. There are restaurants, a food court, movie theatres and, frequently, visiting exhibits and onstage entertainment.

6 Market Square. 2050 Lawrenceville Highway. One of Atlanta's older malls, convenient to Decatur, Clarkston and Tucker, Market Square underwent a facelift recently as well as a name change for the old North DeKalb Mall. Market Square is home to anchors Rich's, Mervyn's and Phar-Mor. Two stores that differ a bit from the usual are the Aviarium, which carries exotic birds and fish and the Everything's A Dollar store, a modern day substitute for the almost anachronistic dime store.

7 Northlake Mall. Located off LaVista Rd. and I-285 at 4800 Briarcliff Rd., this mall is anchored by JC Penney, Macy's and Sears. Shoppers find their favorite chain stores and all manner of merchandise here. Additional shopping areas can be found in the nearby Northlake Festival and Briarcliff Village.

❽ Peachtree Center. 225 Peachtree St. at International Blvd. Three levels of shops, services and food establishments are connected to major downtown hotels and the Merchandise Mart by glassed-in bridges. Frabel's has classic glass sculptures; Puttin' on the Glitz, ladies' high-quality fashion accessories; and International Records, an eclectic selection of tapes and CDs.

❾ Perimeter Mall. Macy's, JC Penney and Rich's anchor this popular northeast mall at 4400 Ashford-Dunwoody Rd. (off I-285 near the Ravinia complex). In addition to a number of national chain stores, Perimeter has interesting gift shops and specialty merchandise. Rich's only Furniture Showroom is located here.

❿ Phipps Plaza. Across from Lenox Square and adjacent to the Ritz-Carlton Hotel of Buckhead, Phipps Plaza is an upscale mall featuring Saks Fifth Avenue, Lord & Taylor, Tiffany & Co., Abercrombie & Fitch, Caswell & Massey, Lillie Rubin and others. The boutique atmosphere and top-of-the-line merchandise attract many Atlantans as well as visitors in search of the perfect gift or the latest in fashion.

⓫ Shannon Southpark Mall. Off I-85 South at Exit #13, Union City, and just five minutes south of Hartsfield International Airport is Shannon Southpark Mall. Major retailers include Macy's, Mervyn's, Rich's and Sears. More than 100 specialty shops include Wrangler Wranch, which sells Western boots, jeans, shirts and accessories for men and women. The Garden Cafe, with its palm-shaded tables, provides an oasis for the foot-weary shopper.

⓬ South DeKalb Mall. Off I-20 at Candler Rd. on the southwest edge of Decatur, this established mall is anchored by JC Penney and Rich's. Oak Tree is a popular men's apparel shop.

13 Southlake Mall. Off I-75 at the Morrow exit, outside I-285, Southlake's major stores are Rich's, Macy's, Sears and JC Penney. Primarily dominated by chain stores, it attracts customers from Forest Park, Riverdale, Fayetteville, Hapeville and points south of downtown.

14 Town Center at Cobb. Anchored by Macy's, Mervyn's, Rich's and Sears, this relatively new mall is located at 400 Barrett Pkwy. in Kennesaw. Merchandise in the locally-owned and chain stores ranges from gag gifts and cookies to clothing and pets.

15 West End Mall. 850 Oak St. S.W. (bounded by Lee, Gordon and Ashby Sts). This older mall, where Sears is the major store, offers apparel and accessories for women, men and children in popular price ranges. There are also eating establishments, record stores and hair salons.

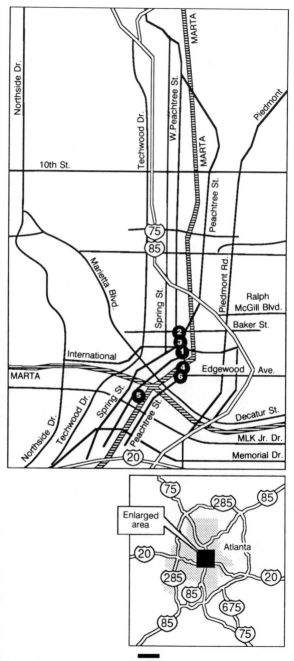

DOWNTOWN

Although the downtown skyscape has changed dramatically in recent years, some of the stores that welcomed customers to Atlanta decades ago are still open for business. Some favorite downtown shopping haunts are included here.

❶ Brooks Brothers. 134 Peachtree St. (near the Equitable Building), 577-4040. Catering to conservative tastes, Brooks Brothers appeals to men and women who appreciate traditional cuts and fabrics. A branch is located at Lenox Square. Hours: 10 a.m.-5:30 p.m, Monday-Saturday.

❷ H. Stockton. 210 Peachtree St., 523-7741. Offering conservative but stylish menswear and furnishings, Stockton also has branches at various mall locations in the metro area. Hours: 9 a.m.-6 p.m., Monday-Friday and 9:30 a.m.-2 p.m., Saturday. Early morning shopping appointments can be arranged by calling the store.

❸ Macy's. 180 Peachtree St., 221-7221. In 1985, Atlanta-based Davison's was completely renovated and became a part of the Macy's chain. Merchandise ranges from gourmet foods to clothing, shoes, cosmetics and jewelry. Macy's anchors a number of malls in the metro area. Hours: 10 a.m.-6 p.m., Monday-Saturday, 10 a.m.-7 p.m., Thursday and 12:30-6 p.m., Sunday.

❹ Muse's. 52 Peachtree St., near Five Points, 522-5400. Long a favorite among Atlanta shoppers, Muse's features traditional men's clothing, shoes, hats and furnishings. Women's suits, dresses and casualwear are also available. Branch stores are located at various malls in the metro area. Hours: 9:30 a.m.-5:30 p.m., Monday-Friday and 10 a.m.-4 p.m., Saturday.

❺ Rich's. 45 Broad St. at Five Points, 586-4636. This famous Atlanta department store features men's, women's and children's fashions. Small housewares are available at the downtown location. The Perimeter Mall Rich's includes their Furniture Showroom which carries home furnishings and appliances. Rich's anchors various malls throughout the Atlanta area. Hours: 10 a.m.-6 p.m., Monday-Saturday.

6 Spencer's Ltd. 84 Peachtree St., Suite 600 (near Five Points), 525-5022. Located in the historic Flat Iron Building, this English-style shop has been serving Atlantans since 1948. In addition to their made-to-measure and mail-order clothing, they also sell ready-made men's garments. Hours: 9 a.m.-5 p.m., Monday-Friday.

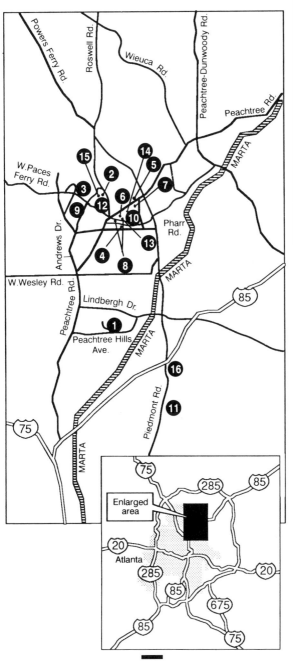

141

BUCKHEAD

Buckhead is an old shopping and residential district, rather sprawling within its parameters, whose major business district is located approximately 6 miles northeast of downtown Atlanta. As home to many of Atlanta's old guard, some of the most impressive homes in Atlanta (including the Governor's Mansion) are located in this area. The Buckhead shops reflect the urbane, elite, and expensive tastes of the customers. Among the specialty shops and boutiques, however, there are a lot of gems to be discovered, and occasionally, even a bargain to be found.

Shopping at a Glance

ANTIQUES AND INTERIOR FURNISHINGS

Map	Location
1 Axis Twenty	200 Peachtree Hills Ave.
2 Country French Connection	3211 Cains Hill Pl. N.W.
3 Pierre Deux	111 W. Paces Ferry Rd.
4 The Potted Plant	3165 E. Shadowlawn Ave. N.E.

JEWELRY & GIFTS

Map	Location
5 Beverly Bremer Silver Shop	3164 Peachtree Rd. N.E.
6 Graveline Metal Gallery	Ste. 27, Andrews Sq. Shopping Ctr.
7 Maier & Berkele	3225 Peachtree Rd.
8 Paces Papers	271 E. Paces Ferry Rd.
9 Swan Coach House Gift Shop	3130 Slaton Dr.
10 Charles Willis	465 E. Paces Ferry Rd.

CLOTHING

Map	Location
11 Bennie's Shoes	2581 Piedmont Rd. N.E.
12 Celebrity on Paces	99 W. Paces Ferry Rd.
13 Jerome's	273 E. Paces Ferry Rd.
14 Regenstein's	3165 Peachtree Rd.
15 Snappy Turtle	110 E. Andrews Dr. N.W.

MISCELLANEOUS

Map	Location
16 Miami Circle shops	Miami Circle N.E.

ANTIQUES & INTERIOR FURNISHINGS

1 Axis Twenty. 200 Peachtree Hills Ave., 261-4022. Contemporary one-of-a-kind and current production furnishings, light fixtures and art objects from the twentieth century including lines such as ARC International, Herman Miller and Patrick Naggar. Hours: 9:30 a.m.-5 p.m., Monday-Friday and Saturday by appointment.

2 Country French Connection. 3211 Cains Hill Pl. N.W., 237-4907. The city's best selection of D. Porthault linens can be found in this retail shop. Antiques, dinnerware and select decorative accessories are also sold. Hours: 10 a.m.-5 p.m., Monday-Saturday.

3 Pierre Deux. 111 W. Paces Ferry Rd., 262-7790. Brightly colored Provencal print fabrics, apparel and gift items. Hours: 10 a.m.-6 p.m., Monday-Saturday.

4 The Potted Plant. 3165 E. Shadowlawn Ave., N.E., 233-7800. A greenhouse with leafy and flowering plants is only a small part of this shop which carries everything from gardening books, decorative items and cache pots to potpourri and imported fabrics. Hours: 9:30 a.m.-5 p.m., Monday-Friday and 9 a.m.-5 p.m., Saturday.

JEWELRY & GIFTS

5 Beverly Bremer Silver Shop. 3164 Peachtree Rd., N.E., 261-4009. A mecca of discontinued, hard-to-find silver patterns and objects — including coffee and tea services — and unusual new finds. Hours: 10 a.m.-5 p.m., Monday-Saturday.

6 Graveline Metal Gallery. Suite 27 at Andrews Square Shopping Center, 237-7422. Custom-crafted and commissioned sterling silver jewelry, flatware and holloware. Hours: 10 a.m.-6 p.m., Tuesday-Saturday.

7 Maier & Berkele. 3225 Peachtree Rd., 261-4911. Atlanta's traditional jeweler for over 100 years has five branch stores in the metro area featuring tasteful selections of china, stemware, watches, gift items and fine jewelry. Hours: 9:45 a.m.-5:30 p.m., Monday-Saturday.

8 Paces Papers. 271 E. Paces Ferry Rd., 231-1111. Elegant to clever stationery, wrapping paper, gifts and cards and custom writing papers, invitations, cards with corporate or personal logos and monograms. Hours: 10 a.m.-5:30 p.m., Monday-Saturday.

9 Swan Coach Gift Shop. 3130 Slaton Dr., 261-0224. A historic, 1928 structure that was originally on the Inman estate. Now owned and operated by the Forward Arts Foundation, it is filled with children's gifts, antique knickknacks, furnishings and housewares. Hours: 10 a.m.-4 p.m., Monday-Saturday.

10 Charles Willis. 465 E. Paces Ferry Rd., 233-9487. A tempting selection of fine jewelry and gift items. Bridal business is always brisk here. Hours: 10 a.m.-5:30 p.m., Monday-Saturday.

CLOTHING

11 Bennie's Shoes. 2581 Piedmont Rd. N.E., 262-1966. A fixture in Atlanta since 1916, this popular men's shoe store carries brand names at discount prices. Two other Atlanta locations. Hours: 8 a.m.-6 p.m., Monday-Saturday.

12 Celebrity on Paces. 99 W. Paces Ferry Rd., 237-5565. Accessories and distinctive designer gowns for evening and dressy daytime wear; mother-of-the bride apparel, too. Hours: 10 a.m.-5 p.m., Monday-Saturday.

⓭ Jerome's. 273 E. Paces Ferry Rd., 264-1284. Contemporary weekend and daytime separates and dresses with an eclectic blend of artwork, sterling collectibles, bed linens, imaginative tablewear and knickknacks. Hours: 11 a.m.-7 p.m., Monday-Saturday and 1-5 p.m., Sunday.

⓮ Regenstein's. 3165 Peachtree Rd., 261-8520. Established in 1878, Regenstein's carries everything from sportswear to furs. This couture shop for women is a favorite among older women in Atlanta. Hours: 10 a.m.-6 p.m., Monday-Saturday.

⓯ Snappy Turtle. 110 E. Andrews Dr., N.W., 237-8341. A boutique specializing in traditional women's clothes and featuring designer lines. A popular shop with locals. Hours: 10 a.m.-5:30 p.m., Monday-Saturday.

MISCELLANEOUS

⓰ Miami Circle. Off Piedmont Ave. at the viaduct next to Buckhead Crossing shopping center. A familiar street to Atlanta decorators, many of the outlets are open to the general public as well. Once a drab and sequestered warehouse district, the street has adapted a neo-Art Deco look and is lined with antique importers. Joseph Konrad is a well-known name for antiques in Atlanta, while Books & Cases offers antique books and maps. A colorful selection of Haitian art can be found at Le Primitif.

DECATUR SHOPPING MAP

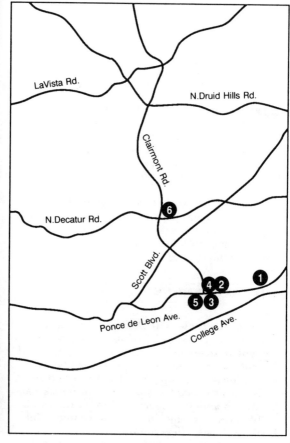

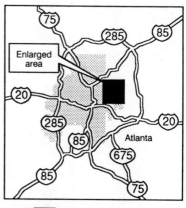

146

DECATUR

Only a few miles due east of downtown Atlanta, Decatur has established residential neighborhoods and a small-town feeling despite the amazing growth beyond its borders.

① DeKalb Farmers Market. 3000 E. Ponce de Leon Ave., 377-6400. Expansive global selection of fresh produce, meat, fish, poultry, canned and processed foods. A bakery and floral shop are also on the premises. Hours: 10-a.m.-9 p.m. Monday-Friday; 9 a.m.-9 p.m. Saturday and Sunday.

② The Family Jewels. 114 E. Ponce de Leon Ave., 377-3774. Antique jewelry and accessories, paintings, pottery, mesh/beaded bags and prints create an eclectic and intriguing blend. Hours: 11 a.m.-9 p.m. Monday-Friday; 2 p.m.-9 p.m Saturday.

③ Good-Bye Girl Antiques. 308-H W. Ponce de Leon Ave., 378-6199. Fine antiques, gifts and interior design services. Hours: 10:30 a.m.-5:30 p.m. Monday-Friday; 10 a.m.-4 p.m. Saturday.

④ Seventeen Steps. 112 E. Ponce de Leon Ave., 377-7564. Choose from inexpensive to moderately expensive items, including museum reproductions, soaps and perfumes, boutique-type items, seasonal merchandise and unusual, fun gifts. Hours: 11 a.m.-8 p.m. Monday-Friday; 11 a.m.-6 p.m. Saturday.

⑤ Sharian. 368 W. Ponce de Leon Ave., 373-2274. Family-owned Sharian stocks a variety of hand-knotted oriental rugs—antiques, semi-antiques, and modern. Hours: 9 a.m.-5 p.m. Monday-Friday and 9 a.m.-1 p.m. Saturday.

⑥ Smoky Mountain Sports. 1373 Clairmont Road, 325-5295. Paradise for outdoor types. Hours: 10 a.m.-7 p.m. Monday-Friday; 10 a.m.-6 p.m. Saturday; and 1-5 p.m. Sunday.

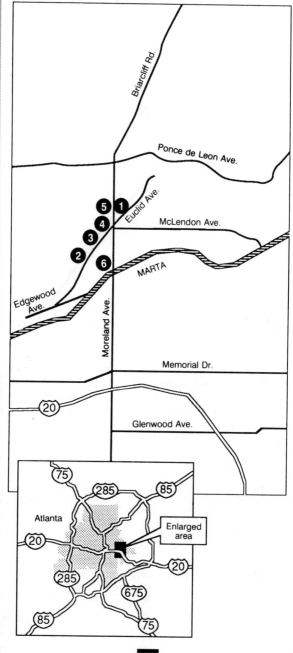

LITTLE FIVE POINTS

In the 1920s and 1930s, the intersection of Euclid and Moreland avenues was a chic shopping spot for aristocratic Inman Park and Druid Hills. Later, the hippies found a haven for themselves here. Now, the district is filled with post-hippies and current counter-culture types. Venture into the neighborhood for a look at the vintage clothing, a stop at the health food grocery, a taste of ethnic food, and an eyeful of local color.

❶ abbadabba's. 421 Moreland Ave. N.E., 588-9577. Clothing, shoes (including Rockport and Birkenstock sandals), and jewelry with a funky flair. Hours: 11 a.m.-7 p.m., Monday-Saturday and 1-6 p.m., Sunday.

❷ The Junkman's Daughter. 1130 Euclid Ave., 577-3188. T-shirts, used costume jewelry, hats, shoes, sunglasses and clothing for men and women. Hours: 11 a.m.-7 p.m., Monday-Saturday and noon-6 p.m., Sunday.

❸ Rene Rene. 1142 Euclid Ave., 522-7363. Avant-garde clothes for women (sizes small-large) designed and manufactured by Rene Sanning. Buckhead branch at 3097 Peachtree Rd., 266-0495. Hours: 11 a.m.-7 p.m., Monday-Friday and 1-5 p.m., Saturday.

❹ Stefan's. 1160 Euclid Ave., 688-4929. "Vintage" garments for men and women, day and evening wear. Clothes, hats and jewelry from the 1890s to the 1950s. Hours: 11 a.m.-7 p.m., Monday-Saturday and noon-6 p.m., Sunday.

❺ Wax 'N' Facts. 432 Moreland Ave., 525-2275. New and used albums, cassettes and CDs at cost-conscious prices for music buffs. Hours: noon-7:30 p.m., Monday-Saturday.

❻ The Wrecking Bar. 292 Moreland Ave., near Euclid Ave., 525-0468. Atlanta's original storehouse of architectural antiques including old mantelpieces, woodwork, glass and other building ornamentations. Hours: 9 a.m.-5 p.m., Monday-Saturday.

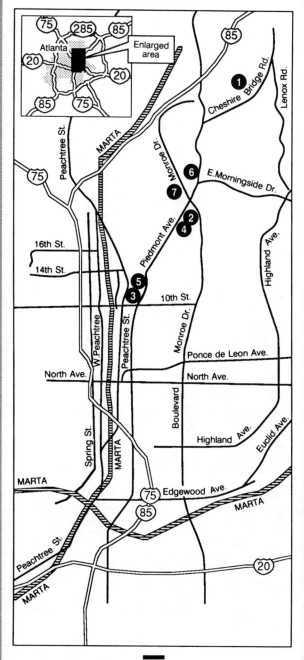

MIDTOWN

Midtown, once recognized as the Haight-Ashbury area of Atlanta, has certainly changed its image in the last several decades. With the incursion of corporate America, the shopping, as well as the scenery, has changed. There is more to Midtown than Peachtree St., however, and some of the more interesting spots are reminiscent of the once-funky Midtown.

1 Atlanta Doll. 2000 Cheshire Bridge Rd. N.E., 248-1151. This shop specializes in collectors' and better brand dolls, those restored and repaired, and dollhouses and miniatures. Hours: 10 a.m.-6 p.m., Monday-Friday; noon-5 p.m., Saturday and Sunday.

2 Costume Architects. 1536 Monroe Dr., 875-6275. Rentable, original costumes such as King Tut and Patty Picnic along with Southern belle gowns, Confederate soldier uniforms and ballgowns. Hours: Monday-Friday 9 a.m.-7 p.m.; Saturday, 10 a.m.-6 p.m.

3 Elysium. 190 10th St. N.E., 875-2060. From earrings and necklaces to rings and bracelets, one finds a wide array of mid-priced jewelry and miscellaneous gifts here. Elysium imports sterling silver items from Mexico and Peru. They also handle Navajo Indian, Marcasites, Alpaca-abalone inlay and ethnic jewelry. Hours: 11 a.m.-6 p.m., Monday-Saturday.

4 Illumina. 1529 Piedmont Ave. N.E., 875-7617. Originally designed jewelry, paintings, masks, crystals and minerals are sold at this intriguing Midtown store. Hours: 11 a.m.-7 p.m., Monday-Saturday.

5 Skate Escape. 1086 Piedmont Ave. across from Piedmont Park, 892-1292. Bike and skating equipment and gear, including sport clothing, is available. Hours: 10 -a.m.-7 p.m., Monday-Friday;

10 a.m.-6 p.m., Saturday; and noon-6 p.m., Sunday.

6 Southern Exposure. 1620 Piedmont Ave. N.E., 875-2669. Designer-quality, showroom-type merchandise offered to the retail market. Home furnishings and accessories, interior design services and artwork are available. Hours: 10 a.m.-5 p.m., Tuesday-Saturday.

7 The Toy Store. 1544 Piedmont Rd., #218 in Ansley Mall, 875-1137. A wide selection of top-of-the-line children's games, toys and dolls including Playmobile, Brio, Carolle, Madame Alexander, Darda, Gund, Gotz and more. Hours: Monday-Saturday, 10 a.m.-6 p.m.

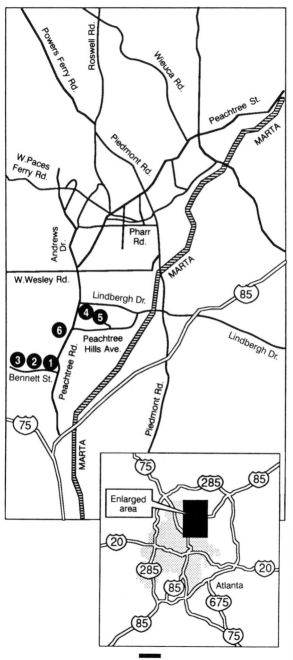

153

PEACHTREE CORRIDOR

The Peachtree Corridor is a three-mile stretch of shops and restaurants which connects Midtown with Buckhead's main business district. In close proximity to Piedmont Hospital and many professional buildings, the Corridor hums with activity, especially during the lunch-time hours.

1 Donatelli. 2140 Peachtree Rd. in Brookwood Square, 350-9154. Imported Italian ceramics for the table and home. Hours: 10 a.m.-6 p.m. Monday-Saturday.

2 Folk-Art Imports Gallery. 25 Bennett St. N.W., 352-2656. Specializes in imported items from Central and South America from rugs and large art pieces to jewelry. Hours: noon-5 p.m. Tuesday-Friday; 11 a.m.-5 p.m. Saturday.

3 Kleinberg Sherrill. 55 Bennett St., 355-2778. Retail boutique for designer line of ladies' handbags, belts, small leather goods and jewelry. Men's small leather goods and belts are also available. Hours: 9:30 a.m.-6 p.m.

4 A Razmataz Child. 2391 Peachtree Rd. N.E., 261-7008. A children's boutique with preemie sizes to girls' and boys' wear. A wonderful selection of domestic and imported toys, dolls, children's accessories, and infant gifts. Hours: 10 a.m.-6 p.m. Monday-Saturday.

5 Dorothy H. Travis Interiors Inc. 12 Kings Circle at Peachtree Hills Ave., 233-7207. Original antique furnishings of primarily French and English origin. Hours: 9:30 a.m.-5 p.m. Monday-Friday.

6 **2300 Peachtree Rd.** A European atmosphere arises from the cobblestone courtyard and the two-story stone buildings. The 20-odd shops include Jane J. Marsden Antiques, Golden Fleece Jewelry Ltd., Jacqueline Adams Antiques/ Interiors, and Yellow House Antiques.

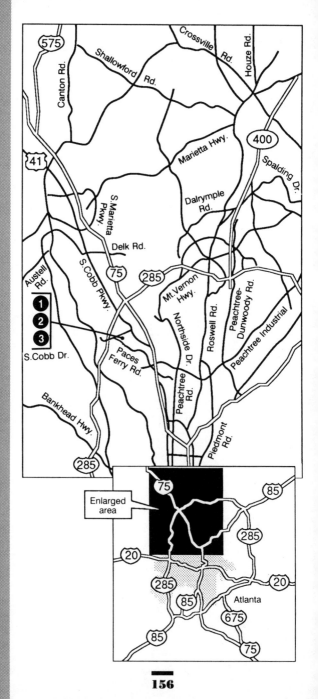

VININGS

Once little and quaint, with a mountain-village atmosphere of hilly terrain and narrow, winding roads, Vinings has become an elite and chic shopping and residential area. Although some of its charm is a thing of the past, it remains an ever-popular area with affluent Northwest Atlantans.

❶ Antique Crossing. 4200 Paces Ferry Rd. N.W., Vinings Jubilee, Ste. 125, 438-8022. This Vinings shop features antique furniture of English and American origin, decorative accessories, crystal, lamps, porcelain and mirrors. Hours: 10 a.m.-6 p.m. Monday-Saturday.

❷ M.L. Jarvis. 4200 Paces Ferry Rd. N.W., Vinings Jubilee, 435-5509. Fun-themed gift shop of personal and playful items suitable for every member of the family. Also a wide selection of stationery. Hours: 10 a.m.-6 p.m. Monday-Saturday.

❸ Vinings General Store. 4200 Paces Ferry Rd. N.W., 432-8044. Gifts of all types in this mishmash of merchandise. Art collectibles and gardening items along with more mundane merchandise such as hardware, cards, and pantyhose. Hours: 9 a.m.-6 p.m. Monday-Saturday; noon-6 p.m., Sunday.

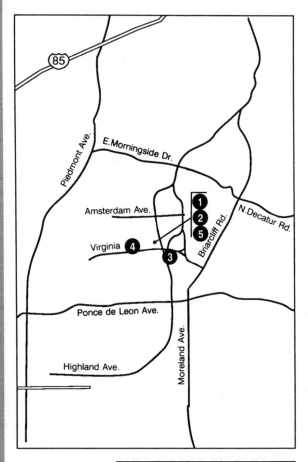

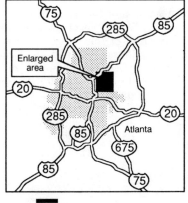

VIRGINIA-HIGHLAND

In the 1920s and 1930s Virginia-Highland was an up-and-coming intown neighborhood with its own strip of shops. In the late 1970s, after a sleepy few decades, the Virginia-Highland area began a rebirth which continues today. Young professionals are not only refurbishing houses but are also bringing trendy revitalization to the old shopping area. Restaurants and shops entice Atlantans throughout the metro area. Stores begin at the Ponce de Leon corner of North Highland and continue northward to Morningside.

1 Babes in Highland. 1030 N. Highland Ave., 876-2448. Here is 100 percent cotton clothing for children, sizes preemie-7, diaper wraps, fun, educational toys and children's accessories. Hours: 11 a.m.-7 p.m., Monday; 11 a.m.-9 p.m., Tuesday-Friday; and noon-6 p.m., Saturday.

2 Mitzi & Romano. 1038 N. Highland Ave., 876-7228. Women's and men's throw-and-go contemporary casualwear. Buckhead branch, East Village Square, 247 Buckhead Ave. N.W., Ste. 104, 237-7653. Hours: 11 a.m.-8 p.m., Monday-Thursday; 11 a.m.-10 p.m., Friday and Saturday; and noon-6 p.m., Sunday.

3 Mooncakes. 1019 Virginia Ave., 892-8043. Whimsical, playfully feminine women's wear for bedtime, daytime and evening. Hours: 11 a.m.-9:30 p.m., Monday-Saturday.

4 Porters. 994 Virginia Ave., 874-7834. Women's and men's clothing and accessories with a contemporary flair. Hours: 11 a.m.-9 p.m., Tuesday-Thursday; 11 a.m.-10 p.m., Friday-Saturday; and 12:30-6 p.m., Sunday.

5 20th-Century Antiques. 1044 N. Highland Ave. N.E., 892-2065. Home furnishings, antique jewelry, antiques, stained glass, southwestern, Art Deco and Art Nouveau decorative items. Hours: 11 a.m.-7 p.m., Monday-Wednesday; 11 a.m.-9 p.m., Thursday-Saturday; and noon-6 p.m., Sunday.

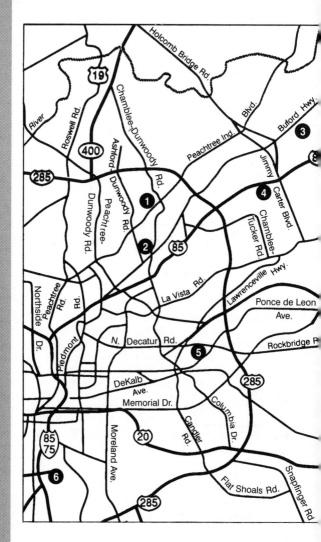

FLEA MARKETS

Flea markets of all sizes and refinements abound in the Atlanta metro area. Many areas outside the perimeter, not mentioned here, are just as worthy of perusal, whether you are in search of a great bargain or just a diversion.

❶ Atlanta Flea Market and Antique Center. 5360 Peachtree Industrial Blvd., Chamblee, 458-0456. Compare the antiques, collectibles and glassware of these permanent exhibitors. Hours: noon-8 p.m. Friday and Saturday; noon-7 p.m. Sunday.

❷ Buford Highway Flea Market. 5000 Buford Hwy., Chamblee, 493-7348. Ethnic merchandise from all over the world can be found here. For example, King Tut Souvenirs imports jewelry from Egypt, with some pieces copied from ancient jewelry. Hours: 11 a.m.-9:30 p.m. Friday and Saturday; noon-7 p.m. Sunday.

❸ Elco Antique Fair. Elco Exhibition Center, 5300 E. Goshen Springs Rd. N.W., Norcross, 279-7349. Spend a day browsing at this show held every second weekend of the month. Hours: 8:30 a.m.-8 p.m. Friday; 9:30 a.m.-6 p.m. Saturday; 10 a.m.-6 p.m., Sunday. Cost: $2 for adults.

❹ Georgia Antique Center and International Market. 6624 I-85 (Between I-285 and Jimmy Carter Blvd. on I-85 N. Access Rd.), Norcross, 446-9292. A large variety of antiques, brass, jewelry and crafts is available at this market. Businesses with outside accesses are open daily, but the interior of the building is open on weekends only. Hours: noon-7 p.m. Friday; 10 a.m.-8 p.m. Saturday; and noon-7 p.m., Sunday.

❺ Kudzu Flea Market. 2874 E. Ponce de Leon Ave., 373-6498. An old building filled with a variety of used and new merchandise is a fun place to browse in Decatur. Hours: front showroom open 10 a.m.-5 p.m. Tuesday-Sunday. Weekend market open 10:30 a.m.-5:30 p.m. Friday and Saturday; 12:30-5:30 p.m. Sunday.

❻ Lakewood Antique Market. 200 Lakewood Ave. S.W. (at the old Lakewood Fairgrounds), 627-2299. On the second weekend of every month you can spend the day enjoying the melange of antiques and collectibles in the several buildings and the outdoor market. Hours: 9 a.m.-8 p.m. Friday and 9 a.m.-6 p.m. Saturday and Sunday. Cost: $2 admission for the weekend; free for children under 12.

RECREATION AND SPORTS

With its full gamut of professional sports, Atlanta attracts visitors from all over who are fans of the Braves, the Hawks, the Falcons and the Attack. Visitors can also take advantage of a plethora of recreational activities and amateur sports opportunities.

Within these pages you will find a variety of recreational and sports opportunities in the metro area. Travel west to Birmingham, a couple of hours away, for horse racing with parimutuel betting or north to try out the ski slopes at Sky Valley in the Georgia Mountains. The North Georgia Mountains also offer these other outdoor sports: horseback riding, kayaking and rafting, fishing, rappelling, spelunking, and camping. Nearby lakes offer a wide variety of water sports.

SPECTATOR SPORTS

HOME TEAMS

Atlanta Attack. Professional soccer games are played at the Omni Coliseum, CNN Center. Call 249-6400 for ticket information.

Atlanta Braves. Atlanta's professional baseball team plays its games at Atlanta-Fulton County Stadium. For tickets, call 522-7630.

Atlanta Falcons. Games take place at Atlanta-Fulton County Stadium. For tickets, call 261-5400.

Atlanta Hawks. The games of Atlanta's professional basketball team are held at the Omni Coliseum at CNN Center. Call 249-6400 for ticket information.

Tickets for all four teams are available through Ticketmaster, 249-6400.

EVENTS

The Atlanta Steeple Chase. A thoroughbred horse race over brush jumps is held annually in April near Cumming. Begun in 1966, the event benefits the Atlanta Speech School. Call 237-7436 for ticket information.

BellSouth Atlanta Golf Classic. This PGA tournament is held in May at the Atlanta Country Club, Marietta. Call 951-8777 for more information.

Georgia State Future's Championship. Laurel Park/Tennis Center, Manning Rd., Marietta, 429-4215. Summer.

Georgia State Junior Open Championships. South Fulton Tennis Center, 5645 Mason Rd., College Park, 306-3059. Summer.

Southern 16 Closed Championships. South Fulton Tennis Center, 5645 Mason Rd., College Park, 306-3059. Summer.

USTA Girls' 14 National Championships. South Fulton Tennis Center. Summer.

CAR RACING

Atlanta International Dragway. Ridgeway Rd., Commerce, 335-2301.

Atlanta International Raceway. Hwy. 41, Hampton, 946-4211. Stock cars and other high-performance-style race cars.

Road Atlanta. Hwy. 53, Braselton, 881-8233. Sports-car racing.

FITNESS

Bally's Holiday. 3270 S. Cobb Dr. S.E., 434-8024. (Nine other metro locations.) Nautilus, indoor track, indoor pool, whirlpool, aerobics, racquetball, steam and sauna, private exercise area for women. Facilities vary by location. Free of charge to members of any Bally's Holiday Fitness Center. Hours: 6 a.m.-10 p.m.; weekdays; 10 a.m.-8 p.m., Saturday; and 10 a.m.-6 p.m., Sunday.

Corporate Fitness Center. 209 Peachtree St. N.E. ($\frac{1}{2}$ block south of the Hyatt Regency Hotel), 525-1210. Nautilus, free weights, aerobics studio, life cycles. Fee is $5 for guests of local hotels. Hours: 11:30 a.m.-8 p.m. Another location is Wildwood Athletic Club, 2300 Windy Ridge Pkwy., Marietta, 953-2120.

Marriott Marquis Health Club. 265 Peachtree Center, 521-0000. Universal weights, indoor and outdoor pools, hydrotherapeutic whirl-pool, life cycles, sauna and steam for men, sauna for women. Free of charge to Marriott Marquis guests. $10 for guests of any other local hotel. Hours: 6 a.m.-11 p.m., weekdays; 7 a.m.-10 p.m., weekends. Pool opens at 7 a.m.

YMCA Downtown Branch. 145 Luckie St., N.W., 527-7676. Nautilus, free weights, Universal weights, basketball court, aerobics classes, two indoor jogging tracks, four racquetball/handball courts, indoor pool, massages, lockers, steam and sauna for men, sauna for women. Hours: 6 a.m.-9 p.m., weekdays; 9 a.m.-6 p.m., Saturday. Eight other metro locations.

RUNNING AND BICYCLING

Chattahoochee River National Recreation Area. A beautiful series of parklands, administered by the National Park Service, along a 48-mile stretch of the Chattahoochee River. Call 394-8335 for locations and information about the numerous trails along the forest floor or the river's edge. The park's 3.1-mile loop is a popular running trail.

Fernbank Science Center. 156 Heaton Park Dr. N.E., 378-4311. A two-mile paved trail through one of the largest virgin forests in any U.S. metro area. Maps available at the gate. Hours: 2-5 p.m., daily; 10 a.m.-5 p.m., Saturday.

Piedmont Park. Piedmont Ave. and 14th St. N.E. Paved trails for walking, bicycling and roll-erskating. Three-mile jogging trail. Soccer and softball fields require reservations. Twelve tennis courts operate on a first-come, first-serve basis. Outdoor swimming pool.

Skate Escape. 1086 Piedmont Ave. N.E., 892-1292. Rentals for cycling and skating in nearby Piedmont Park.

Stone Mountain Park. Seven miles east of I-285 on U.S. 78, Stone Mountain Freeway, 498-5702. Ten miles of scenic hiking trails for both strenuous and non-strenuous walking. A 1.3-mile trail leads to the top of the mountain. Rentals for cycling on paved paths.

GOLF

Municipal courses are open to dusk and reservations may be made by calling 355-1833. The weekday fee is $10.60, weekends $12.72. 18-hole courses. Rental clubs are available. All of the courses are tree-lined on rolling terrain with bermuda grass greens.

9 HOLES
Candler Park Golf Course. 585 Candler Park Dr. S.W., 371-1260. Fees: students and senior citizens, $3.75 weekdays and $4.50 weekends; other adults, $4.25 on weekdays and $5 on weekends.

18 HOLES
Alfred Tup Holmes Golf Course. 2300 Wilson Dr. S.W., 753-6158.

Bobby Jones Golf Course. 384 Woodward Way N.W., 355-1009.

Browns Mill Golf Course. 480 Cleveland Ave. S.E., 366-3573.

North Fulton Golf Course. 216 W. Wieuca Rd. N.E., 255-0723.

OTHER COURSES OPEN TO THE PUBLIC:

The Metropolitan Club of Atlanta. 3000 Fairington Pkwy., Decatur, 981-5325. 18-hole course designed by Bobby Jones. Fees: $31.05, weekdays; $41.05, weekends. Bent grass greens. Rental clubs available.

Stone Mountain Golf Course. Stone Mountain Park, 498-5717. 18-hole championship course designed by Bobby Jones, rated among the "Top 25" public courses in the country by *Golf Digest*. Fees: $32.00 for 18 holes, $16.00 for 9 holes, daily (includes cart).

DRIVING RANGE:

Jim Hearn Golf Center. 4445 Buford Hwy., 455-9731. A 17-acre driving range, open to the public seven days a week, offers three full-time teaching pros, video instruction and golf club repair. Hours: 10:30 a.m.-dark, winter months; 10:30 a.m.-10 p.m., March-October. Cost: $2 for small buckets and $4 for large.

GOLF

TENNIS

Fees on Atlanta area municipal courts range from $1.50 to $2.50 per player. Each center is staffed by a tennis professional.

Bitsy Grant Tennis Center. 2125 Northside Dr. N.W., 351-2774. Thirteen clay, ten hard courts; lights on six clay and four hard courts.

Chastain Park Tennis Center. 110 W. Wieuca Rd. N.E., 255-1993. Nine lighted hard courts.

McGee Tennis Center. 820 Beecher Ct. S.W., 752-7177. Nine hard courts, eight lighted.

North Fulton Tennis Center. 500 Abernathy Rd. N.E., 256-1588. Four clay courts, twenty hard courts; all have lights.

Piedmont Park Tennis Center. Park Dr. N.E., 872-1507. Twelve lighted hard courts.

Washington Park Tennis Center. Lena St. N.W., 523-1169. Eight lighted hard courts.

WATER SPORTS

BOATING, FISHING*, RAFTING, CANOEING

The Chattahoochee River. Flowing from the Georgia mountains to the Gulf of Mexico and winding through the north and northwest sections of Atlanta, "the Hooch" is ideal for rafting and fishing for trout and perch.

The Chattahoochee Outdoor Center. With three sites on the river, this is the official concessionaire for the Chattahoochee River National Recreation Area. Rental rafts, canoes, and kayaks available. Clinics offered in canoeing, kayaking, and fishing. Call 395-6851 for information. Open May to mid-September.

Lake Lanier. A 38,000-acre reservoir 50 miles northeast of the city, Lake Lanier is popular with boaters and fishermen. Crappie, spotted bass, and bream are usual game. Call the U.S. Corps of Engineers, 945-9531, for information about boat ramps and rentals, marinas, camping areas, and picnic facilities.

Lake Lanier Islands. I-85 north to I-985, Exit 1, left on Hwy. 20; follow signs. Main public recreation facility for Lake Lanier. Call 945-6701 for houseboat, pontoon, and fishing boat rentals, bait and gasoline sales, and tackle rental.

Lake Allatoona. Forty miles northwest of Atlanta, this 11,869-acre reservoir on the Etowah River abounds with black crappie, bluegill, and redbreast sunfish. Call the U.S. Corps of Engineers, 688-7870, for information about boat ramps, marinas, camping areas, and picnic facilities.

Stone Mountain Park. Seven miles east of I-285 on U.S. 78, Stone Mountain Freeway, 498-5702. Canoe, rowboat, pedal boat and pontoon rentals are available for use on the 363-acre Stone Mountain Lake and two stocked fishing lakes. $5 park admission per car.

*A Georgia fishing license is required for fresh water fishing. For information contact the Georgia Game and Fish Division, 656-3524.

SWIMMING

Atlanta's major **outdoor** municipal swimming facilities charge $1 for adults and $.50 for children. Call 653-7129 for further listings and hours.

Chastain Memorial Park. 234 W. Wieuca Rd. N.W., 255-0863.

Grant Park. 625 Park Ave. S.E., 622-3041.

Piedmont Park. Piedmont Ave. and 14th St. N.E., 892-0117.

Indoor facilities also charge $1 for adults and $.50 for children.

M.L. King South. 582 Connally St. N.E., 658-6099.

M.L. King North. 70 Boulevard N.E., 688-3791.

MANMADE BEACHES

Lake Lanier Island. Lake Lanier, I-85 north to I-985. Exit 1; left on Hwy. 20; follow signs, 945-6701.

Stone Mountain Park. Seven miles east of I-285 on U.S. 78, Stone Mountain Freeway, 498-5702. Water Works Beach complex. $3 admission for all ages. Hours: 10 a.m.-7 p.m. daily.

MISCELLANEOUS SPORTS AND RECREATION

BOWLING

Express Lanes. 1936 Piedmont Cir. N.E., 874-5703. 32 lanes. Hours: 9 a.m.-4 a.m. daily.

Northeast Plaza Lanes. 3285 Buford Hwy. N.E., 636-7548. Hours: 9 a.m.-midnight, Sunday-Thursday and 9 a.m.-4 a.m., Friday and Saturday.

FLYING

Sky Warriors, Inc. 3996 Aviation Cir. N.W. (Fulton County Airport-Brown Field), 699-7000. A truly unique experience for the highly adventuresome is this four hours in a fighter plane. Passengers act out combat scenarios at the cost of about 70 viewings of *Top Gun*. Office hours: 9 a.m.-5 p.m. daily. Missions take off at 10 a.m. and 2 p.m. Monday-Friday; 7:30 a.m., 10 a.m., and 2 p.m. Saturday and Sunday.

HORSEBACK RIDING

Double TK Ranch. 1231 Shallowford Rd., Marietta, 926-3795. English- and Western-style lessons available. Horses are $13 per hour; ponies for children are $7 per hour. Hours: 10 a.m.-5 p.m., daily.

HOT-AIR BALLOONING

Atlanta Hot Air Promotions. 5455 Buford Hwy., Doraville, 452-0033.

Bulldawg Balloon Tours. 366-5891.

Sundance Balloon. 395 8th St. N.E., 875-3419.

Time Balloons. 997-1444.

ICE SKATING

Parkaire Olympic Ice Arena. 4880 Lower Roswell Rd. N.E., Marietta, 973-0753. Olympic-size rink; rental skates. Call for hours and fees.

Stone Mountain Ice Chalet. Stone Mountain Park. Seven miles east of I-285 on U.S. 78, Stone Mountain Freeway. 10 a.m.-noon and 2-5 p.m., Monday-Friday; 8-10 p.m., Wednesday and Thursday; 8-10:30 p.m, Friday and Saturday; 1-3 p.m. and 3:30-5:30 p.m., Sunday. Cost: $3.50 admission; $1.50 for skate rental.

MINIATURE GOLF

Dilly Dally's Golf and Games. 1927 S. Cobb Dr. S.E., Marietta, 436-0036. Hours: Opens at 2 p.m. Monday-Friday; 11 a.m. on weekends.

Mountasia Fantasy Golf and Games. 175 Barrett Pkwy., Marietta, 422-3440.

Pebble Beach Mini Golf. 4400 Roswell Rd. N.E., Marietta, 973-7828.

Putt-Putt Golf and Games. 3382 Shallowford Rd., Chamblee, 458-0888. Hours: 11 a.m.-11 p.m. Sunday-Thursday; 11 a.m.-midnight Friday; 9 a.m.-midnight on Saturday.

RACQUETBALL

Eastlake Indoor Tennis-Racquetball Center. 2573 Alston Dr. S.E., 373-3500. Hours: 9 a.m.-11 p.m. daily. Cost: $5 per hour for non-members.

ROLLER-SKATING

All American Skating Center. 5400 Bermuda Rd., Stone Mountain, 469-9775.

Roswell Roller Rink. 780 Old Roswell Rd., Roswell, 998-9700.

Screaming Wheels Roller Rink and Bowling. 1724 Stewart Ave. S.W., 752-5595.

SHOOTING

Dekalb County Firing Range. 3905 N. Goddard Rd., Lithonia, 482-8965. Hours: 10 a.m.-6 p.m. Friday, Saturday and Monday. Cost: $7 per hour; trap is $4 per round on Friday and Saturday. No one under 10 admitted. Children under 18 must be accompanied by an adult (age 21 or older). Ranges are 25, 50 and 100 yards. 200-yard ranges available on Saturday.

Wolf Creek Trap and Skeet Range. 3070 Merk Rd. S.W., 346-1545. Ten ranges for trap and skeet. Hours: 1-10 p.m. Tuesday-Friday; 11 a.m.-5 p.m. Saturday and Sunday.

SKYDIVING

Atlanta Skydiving Center. County Line Rd., Jenkinsburg, 775-9150. Skydiving and parachute rides.

TRANSPORTATION

Fortunately for visitors who want a vacation from the automobile (or who choose not to tackle the multi-laned I-285 highway which rings the city) MARTA's rapid-rail and bus system offer transportation almost anywhere inside the perimeter. With the on-going expansion of MARTA and its highway system, Atlanta is preparing for both the influx of visitors during the 1996 Olynpics and the city's continuing growth. Taxis are available for direct-route destinations, while those who wish to travel in style can avail themselves of the city's limousine services. Finally, for a leisurely ride around downtown Atlanta, horse-drawn carriages, romantic and reminiscent of the Old South, provide an engaging diversion on moonlit nights or during the weekend.

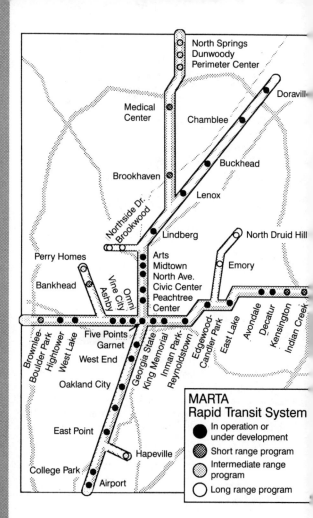

MARTA MAP

MARTA Rapid Transit System

- ● In operation or under development
- ◉ Short range program
- ◎ Intermediate range program
- ○ Long range program

Stations:
North Springs, Dunwoody, Perimeter Center, Doravill, Medical Center, Chamblee, Buckhead, Brookhaven, Lenox, Northside Dr., Brookwood, Lindberg, North Druid Hill, Perry Homes, Arts, Midtown, North Ave., Civic Center, Peachtree Center, Emory, Bankhead, Omni, Vine City, Ashby, North Druid Hill, Five Points, Garnet, Georgia State, King Memorial, Inman Park-Reynoldstown, Edgewood-Candler Park, East Lake, Avondale, Decatur, Kensington, Indian Creek, Brownlee-Boulder Park, Hightower, West Lake, West End, Oakland City, East Point, Hapeville, College Park, Airport

MARTA

The Metropolitan Atlanta Rapid Transit Authority (MARTA), created in 1965, is a wide-reaching public transportation system. The rapid-rail system includes east-west and north-south lines that serve Fulton and DeKalb counties. The main station, Five Points, is located in the heart of downtown off Marietta Street (3 ½ blocks east of the Omni International at CNN Center.) Each station has a name, letter and number code—such as "Lenox N7"—to indicate the direction and number of stops from Five Points. (The station at the CNN Center is Omni Station W1). The rail system also operates a direct route to Hartsfield Airport.

All MARTA stations and rapid-rail cars are accessible to handicapped passengers. Elderly and handicapped passengers may ride with half-fare permits except during morning rush hours. For more information on handicapped services, call 848-3340. Handicapped transportation is also available through Lift-Van; reservations may be made by calling 659-2543. On buses and rails, riders are expected to pay in exact change or tokens, which can be purchased at the various stations.

Other important MARTA numbers:
Airport Service—848-3454
Customer Services and Complaints—848-5022
General Information—848-5000
Lost and Found—848-3208
Schedule Information—848-4711
Stadium/Sports Service—848-3456
Rail Service—848-3450

AIRLINES AND AIRPORTS

Airlines with local offices:
Air Paraguay — 233-2717
Alitalia — 393-9550
American — 521-2655
Atlantic Southeast — 996-4872
British Airways — 1-800-221-1111
Cayman Airways — 457-1687
Continental — 436-3300
Delta — 765-5000
Finnair — 320-9787
Japan Air Lines — 521-1616
Korean Air — 763-0185
KLM — 523-5900
Lufthansa — 266-1616
Pan Am — 1-800-221-1111
Sabena — 524-2598
Scandinavian Airlines — 1-800-221-2350
Singapore Airlines — 577-5644
Swissair — 956-9704
TWA — 522-5738
United — 394-2234
US Air — 1-800-428-4322
Varig Brazilian Airlines — 261-4846

Local Airports:
Hartsfield International Airport
    (Atlanta Airport)
    For flight Information, paging and
        reservations see individual carrier.
    International Information — 530-2081
    Parking — 530-6725

180

Aerospec Inc. Falcon Field Airport/
   Peachtree City — 487-8050
Berry Hill Airport/Stockbridge — 474-5126
Dekalb/Peachtree — 457-7236
Fulton County Airport-
   Charlie Brown Field — 699-4200
McCollum Airport/Marietta — 422-4382
South Expressway Airport/Jonesboro — 471-0534
Stone Mountain Britt Memorial Airport —
   469-7604

Charter and leasing services:
Fees, availability and charges may vary.

Air Charter Association — 239-0781
AAA Charter Co. — 261-4281
Academy Airline — 688-4084
Air Center Gwinnett — 963-6336
Air Charter By Joseph — 452-1745
Air One Inc. — 691-3593
Astro Aero Inc. — 699-7925
Astron Enterprises — 455-3454
Aviation Atlanta — 458-8034
Beechcraft Charter Rental and Leasing
   — 699-9200 or 765-1300 or 454-5010
Colvin Aviation — 458-5100
Dash Air Charter — 355-4272
Dooley Helicopters Inc. — 458-3431
Epps Air Service inc. — 458-9851
Falcon Charter Service Inc. — 457-3301
Flight International of Georgia — 452-0010
Flite Services Inc. — 455-3456
Gem City Aviation Inc. — 422-2345
Hangar One Inc. — 765-1300 or 454-5000 or
   699-9200
Helicopters Inc. — 454-6958
Hill Aircraft and Leasing Corp. — 691-3330
Mid-State/Executive Helicopters Inc. — 564-1901
Old South Aviation Inc. — 458-3633
Peachtree DeKalb Flight Academy — 457-8223
Phoenix Air — 971-8071
Prestige Helicopters — 458-6047
Smith Air Inc. — 477-8888
South Air Aviation Inc. — 487-9502

Cabs, Limos and Carriages

If you want to leave the driving to someone else, here's a list of cab, limousine and horse-drawn carriage companies that operate in the city and are licensed by the city's Taxi and Vehicle-For-Hire Bureau at 818 Washington St. S.W. For additional information call 658-7600.

Cabs:

Waiting time costs $10 an hour. The minimum fare is $1.50 for the first $1/5$ mile and 20 cents for each additional 1/5 mile.

Ace Taxicab Company — 659-8793
All Taxicab Company — 758-8299
American Taxicab Company — 688-5656
Ashby Street Taxicab Company — 586-0728
Atlanta Royal Taxicab — 584-6655
Buckhead Safety Taxicab — 233-1152
Checker Taxicab Company — 351-8255
Citywide Taxicab Company — 875-1223
Colonial Taxicab Company — 351-8255
Courtesy Taxicab Company — 622-5408
Gate City Taxicab Company — 758-6124
Georgia Taxicab Company — 755-1723
London Taxicab Company — 681-2280
Metropolitan Ben Hill Taxicab Company — 349-1147
Million Taxicab Company — 688-9295
National Taxicab Company — 752-6834
Peoples Independent Taxicab Company — 688-8500

Professional Taxicab Company — 522-2227
Quicker Taxicab Company — 522-5894
Rapid Taxicab Company — 755-1723
Safari Taxicab Company — 755-1723
Star Taxicab Company — 758-6616
United Taxicab Company — 658-1638
University Taxicab Company — 522-0200
Wilson Taxicab Company — 523-6414

Limousine Services:

Rental fees for a limo in Atlanta range from $45-$65 per hour.

A. Lawrence Limousine Service — 885-1446
A Atlanta Limousine Service Inc. — 351-5466
A-National Limousine Service — 581-9731
A-l Limousine Service Inc. — 662-6666
Atlanta Livery Limousine Service — 872-8282
Avanti Limousine Service Inc. — 233-6100
Carey of Atlanta — 681-3366
Clark Limousine Service Inc. — 624-4492
Davis Limousine Service — 524-3413
Dynasty Limousine Service — 325-5466 or
   325-4314
Executive Town & Country Service — 763-2225
Greater Atlanta Livery Association — 755-7300
GPM Limousine Service — 355-1634
Kings & Queens Limousine Service — 255-4690
Lowe English Classic Limousine, Inc. — 659-6500
Mercedes Executive Services Inc. — 594-0256
New World Limousine — 622-5445
Northside Limousine Company — 688-7801
Peach State Limousine Service — 948-2520
Phoenix Car and Limousine Service — 876-3041
Premier Limousine Services Inc. — 350-9999
Presidential Limousine Service — 872-7520
Robinson Limousine Inc. — 262-1103
Simon's Stretch Limousine Service — 691-2101
Sims & Son Limousine Service — 987-0249
Tracey's Limousine — 634-8557
Unique Limousine Service — 237-1330
Your Limousine Service — 766-6669

CABS, LIMOS AND CARRIAGES

Horse-drawn Carriage Companies:

The average cost of a carriage ride is $12.50 per person.

Courtesy Carriage Company — 767-3204
Inshirah Stables — 523-3993
Pegasus Carriage Company — 681-3461
VIP Carriage Company — 264-8984

RENTAL CARS

Accent Rent A Car — 961-4477
Action Auto Rental — 669-0041
Advance Leasing & Rent-A-Car — 763-3211
Airport Ford Inc. — 768-5000
Airport Thrifty Car Rental — 761-5286
Agency Rent-A-Car — 991-1274
Alamo Rent-A-Car — 768-4161
Atlanta Rent-A-Car — 763-1160
Avis — 530-2700
Budget — 530-3000
Dollar Rent A Car — 766-0244
Enterprise Leasing/Rent-A-Car — 763-0643
General Rent-A-Car — 763-2035
Hertz — 530-2906
Lemon Rentals — 765-8721
Holiday Payless Rent-A-Car — 763-2038
Major Rent-A-Car — 991-5990
National Car Rental — 530-2800
Payless Car Rental — 763-2038
Replacement Rent-A-Car Inc. — 991-1274
Sears Rent-A-Car — 530-3000
Thrifty Car Rental — 761-5286
Ugly Duckling — 762-3000
USA Rent-A-Car System — 765-8721

CABS, LIMOS AND CARRIAGES / RENTAL CARS

SIGHTSEEING TOURS

Atlanta Convention Planners — 355-8716
Atlanta Preservation Center — 522-4345
Gray Line of Atlanta — 767-0594
Harmon Brothers Charter Inc. — 752-9479
New Georgia Railroad.
   See **UNDERGROUND** or call: — 656-0769
Presenting Atlanta — 231-0200

BUSES AND TRAINS

Greyhound/Trailways — 522-6300
Amtrak
   General Information
     and reservations — 1-800-872-7245
   Passenger paging — 881-3060

USEFUL INFORMATION

Car Assistance:
AAA Florida/Georgia — 875-8484
24-hour emergency road service — 875-7175

Chambers of Commerce:
Atlanta — 586-8403
Clayton County — 478-6549
Cobb County — 980-2000
Conyers-Rockdale — 483-7049
Dekalb County — 378-8000
Douglas County — 942-5022
Fayette County — 461-9983
Gwinnett County — 963-5128
Henry County — 957-5786
North Fulton County — 993-8806
South Fulton County — 964-1984

Delivery Services:
Airborne Express — 761-7199
Courier Dispatch Group — 767-7930
Dependable Courier — 763-1100
DHL Worldwide Express — 997-1635
Executive Courier — 350-2200
Express Mail, U.S. Postal Service — 765-7486
Federal Express — 321-7566
Flash Courier Service Inc. — 873-5052
PDQ Delivery Service — 627-0856
Sonic Delivery — 763-3400

Dental:
Northern District Dental
    Society Referral Service — 270-1635
Georgia Dental Association — 458-6166

Directory Assistance: — 411

Fire: — 911

Florists: Call the Metropolitan
Atlanta Floral Delivery Cooperative
at 577-8551 for a list of local par-
ticipating florists.

Georgia State Parks Information: —
800-342-7275

Legal:
Atlanta Bar Association — 521-0781
Atlanta Bar Association Referral Service —
    521-0777
Legal Aid — 524-5811

Newsstands:
Ansley Mall Bookstore,
    1544 Piedmont Ave. N.E. — 875-6492
B. Dalton Bookseller (downtown)
    Five Points — 659-1330
    Peachtree Center — 577-2555
Borders Book Shop,
    3655 Roswell Rd. — 237-0707
Dixie News Stand,
    13 Decatur St. S.E. — 524-0858

Eastern Newsstand Corporation,
   231 Peachtree St. N.E.—659-5670
   100 Peachtree St. N.E.—522-6859
   3414 Peachtree Rd. N.E. —261-6080
   133 Peachtree St. N.E.—659-2497
   229 Peachtree St. N.E.—521-2099
   3495 Piedmont Rd. N.E.—231-3799
   675 W. Peachtree St. N.E.—872-2645
The News Center,
   4903 Jonesboro, Forest Park—361-9340
Oxford Book Store,
   2345 Peachtree Rd. N.E.—364-2700
   360 Pharr Rd. N.E.—262-3333
   1200 W. Paces Ferry Rd. N.W.—364-2488
Waldenbooks Lenox Square —261-2781
   All other Waldenbooks metro locations, too.

Pharmacy:
Treasury Drugs (Old Plaza Drugs) is open
   24 hours a day at 1061 Ponce de Leon Ave.—
   876-0381

Passport and Visa Information: 765-7324

Police: —911

Road Conditions: —656-5267

Western Union:
20 Forsyth St.—577-6413

Tourist Information:
Atlanta Convention and Visitors Bureau—
   521-6688
Georgia Department of Tourism—656-3590

Time: ($.50 charge)—976-1221

Weather: —936-8550
National Weather Service
   regional forecasts—762-6151

HOSPITALS

Physician referral:
Medical Association of Atlanta — 881-1714

Downtown:
Crawford W. Long Memorial Hospital
of Emory University,
550 Peachtree St. N.E. — 686-4411
Georgia Baptist Medical Center,
300 Boulevard N.E. — 653-4000
Grady Memorial Hospital,
80 Butler St. S.E. — 589-4307

Midtown:
Piedmont Hospital,
1968 Peachtree Rd. N.W. — 350-2222

North:
AMI North Fulton Regional Hospital,
11585 Alpharetta St., Roswell — 751-2500
HCA West Paces Ferry Hospital,
3200 Howell Mill Rd. N.W. — 351-0351
Northside Hospital,
1000 Johnson Ferry Rd. N.E. — 851-8000
Saint Joseph's Hospital,
5665 Peachtree-Dunwoody Rd. N.E. — 851-7001
Scottish Rite Children's Hospital,
1001 Johnson Ferry Rd. N.E. — 256-5252

East:
Dekalb Medical Center,
2701 North Decatur Rd. — 297-2700
Emory Hospital,
1364 Clifton Rd. N.E. — 727-7021
Egleston Hospital for Children,
1405 Clifton Rd. N.E. — 325-6000
Gwinnett Medical Center,
710 West Pike St., Lawrenceville — 995-4321
Humana Hospital,
2160 Fountain Dr., Snellville — 979-0200
Rockdale Hospital,
1412 Milstead Ave., Conyers — 922-8900

Northeast:
Shallowford Community Hospital,
   4575 N. Shallowford Rd., Chamblee — 454-2000

Northwest:
Cobb Medical Center,
   3850 Austell Rd. S.W., Austell — 944-5000
Kennestone Hospital,
   677 Church St. N.E., Marietta — 426-2000

South:
Clayton General Hospital,
   11 S.W. Upper Riverdale Rd., Riverdale —
   991-8000
Henry General Hospital,
   1133 Hudson Bridge Rd., Stockbridge —
   389-2200
South Fulton Medical Center,
   1170 Cleveland Ave., East Point — 699-4000
Southwest Hospital and Medical Center,
   501 Fairburn Rd. S.W. — 699-1111

West:
Douglas General Hospital and Medical Complex,
   8954 Hospital Dr., Douglasville — 949-1500

BOOKSTORES

GENERAL BOOKSTORES

Ansley Mall Bookstore,
   1544 Piedmont Ave. N.E. — 875-6492
Ardmore Book Store, 5980 Roswell Rd. —
   256-4203
B. Dalton Bookseller,
   24 Peachtree Street at Five Points — 659-1337
   231 Peachtree Center — 577-2555
   Also at various mall locations.
Bookland, Shannon Mall — 964-5061
   Banks Crossing Shopping Center,
   Fayetteville — 460-8863
Book Star, 4101 Upper Roswell Rd.,
   Ste. 804, Marietta — 578-4455
Books & Bytes,
   850 Dogwood Rd., Lawrenceville — 985-0812
Books Again, 4920 Roswell Rd. — 847-9107
Borders Book Shop,
   3655 Roswell Rd. N.E. — 237-0707
Brentanos, Perimeter Mall — 394-6658
Cole's, The Book People, Gwinnett Place —
   476-7410
   Town Center at Cobb — 423-1579
   Market Square — 634-2616
Chapter 11, 2107 N. Decatur Rd. — 325-1505
Dollar Bookstore, 2179 Roswell Rd.,
   Marietta — 565-8696
Doubleday Book Shops, Underground — 681-1797
Douglasville Books, 3211 Highway 5 — 949-4363
Fayette Book Shop,
   692 Glynn St., Fayetteville — 461-5907

Final Touch Gallery and Books,
   308 W. Ponce De Leon Ave.,
   Decatur, Ste. F — 378-1462
Little Professor Book Center,
   8337 Roswell Rd., Dunwoody — 992-6283
Little Professor Book Center,
   59 S. Park Square N.E., Marietta — 427-5664
Oxford Book Store,
   2345 Peachtree St. N.E. — 364-2700
   360 Pharr Rd. N.E. — 262-3333
   1200 W. Paces Ferry Rd. N.W — 364-2700
The Renaissance Bookshop,
   595 Piedmont Ave. N.E. — 873-4161
Royal's Books,
   2126 Fountain Square, Snellville — 979-7427
Tall Tales Bookshop, Inc.,
   2999 N. Druid Hills Rd. N.E. — 636-2498
Tattersall's Book Merchants,
   902 Center St., Conyers — 922-1536
Waldenbooks, Lenox Square — 261-2781
   Phipps Plaza — 261-9377
   Also at various other mall locations.

SPECIALTY BOOKSTORES
African American Book Shop,
   1392 Gordon St. S.W. — 755-3756
Architectural Book Center, Colony Square,
   1197 Peachtree St. N.E. — 873-1052
Atlantis Connection (New Age),
   1402 N. Highland Ave. N.E. — 881-6511
Avalon Book Center (New Age),
   375 Pharr Rd. N.E. — 233-1611
The Baptist Book Store,
   2930 Flowers Rd., Chamblee — 458-8131
   4060 Jonesboro Rd., Forest Park — 363-4040
C. Dickens (Antiquarian and Used),
   Lenox Square — 231-3825
Charis Books and More (Feminist),
   419 Moreland Ave. N.E. — 524-0304
Children's Book & Gift Market,
   375 Pharr Rd. N.E. — 261-1211
   or — 261-3442
Cokesbury Books and Church Supplies,
   2495 Lawrenceville Hwy., Decatur — 320-1034

First World Bookstore (African-American),
677 ½ Cascade Ave. S.W. — 758-7124
Greenbriar Mall — 346-3263
Hakim's Book Store (African-American),
842 Martin Luther King, Jr. Dr. S.W. —
221-0740
International Bookstore (Spanish),
3652 Shallowford Rd., Doraville — 457-6737
Koryo Books (Korean),
5181 Buford Hwy., Doraville — 457-6737
Latitudes (Travel Maps), Lenox Square — 237-6144
Perimeter Mall — 394-2772
My Storyhouse (Children's),
3000 Old Alabama Rd., Alpharetta — 664-8697
1401 Johnson Ferry Rd. N.E.,
Marietta — 973-2244
Old New York Book Store
(Antiquarian and Used),
1069 Juniper St. N.E. — 881-1285
The Phoenix and Dragon Bookstore For A
New Age, 300 Hammond Dr. N.E. — 255-5207
Science Fiction and Mystery Book Shop,
752 ½ N. Highland Ave. N.E. — 875-7326
Shrine of the Black Madonna Bookstore
and Culture Center,
946 Gordon St. S.W. — 752-6125
Sphinx Metaphysical Books,
1510 Piedmont Ave. N.E. — 875-2665
Tract Depot-Christian Bookstore,
5547 Peachtree Rd., Chamblee — 457-8048
U.S. Government Bookstore,
275 Peachtree St. N.E. — 331-6947
World Journal Chinese Bookstore,
5389 New Peachtree Rd., Chamblee — 451-4509

MEDIA

NEWSPAPERS

Daily:

The Atlanta Daily World, 145 Auburn Ave. N.E., 659-1110.

The Atlanta Journal and The Atlanta Constitution, 72 Marietta St. N.W., 526-5151.

Clayton News Daily, 138 Church St., Jonesboro, 478-5753.

The Gwinnett Daily News, 200 Hampton Green N.W., Duluth, 381-8535.

The Marietta Daily Journal, 580 Fairground St. S.E., Marietta, 428-9411.

Rockdale Citizen, 969 Main St., Conyers, 483-7108.

USA Today, 1611 W. Peachtree St. N.E., 874-4221.

TELEVISION STATIONS - VHF

2 WSB (ABC) 1601 W. Peachtree St. N.E., 897-7000.
5 WAGA (CBS) 1551 Briarcliff Rd. N.E., 875-5551.
8 WGTV (PBS) 1540 Stewart Ave. S.W., 756-4700.
11 WXIA (NBC) 1611 W. Peachtree St. N.E., 892-1611.

TELEVISION STATIONS - UHF

17 WTBS (Ind.) 1050 Techwood Dr. N.W.
30 WPBA (PBS) 740 Bismark Rd. N.E.,
875-5551.
36 WATL (Ind./Fox) One Monroe Place,
881-3600.
46 WGNX (Ind.) 1810 Briarcliff Rd. N.E.,
325-4646.
69 WVEU (Ind.) 2700 N.E. Expwy., A-700,
325-6929.
CNN (Ind.) One CNN Center N.W., 827-1500.

RADIO STATIONS

Adult Contemporary: WZAL (1410 AM),
WSTR (94.1 FM), WSB (98.5 FM), WMKJ (96.7
FM), WALR (104.7 FM).

Business-talk: WFOM (1230 AM).

Country: WHNE (1170 AM), WKHX (101.5
FM), WYAI (104 FM), WCHK (105 FM), WYAY
(106.7 FM).

Christian and Gospel: WAEC (860 AM),
WNIV (970 AM), WGUN (1010 AM), WTJH (1260
AM), WXLL (1310 AM), WAOK (1380 AM), WAVO
(1420 AM), WYZE (1480 AM), WYNX (1550 AM),
WSSA (1570 AM), WWEV (91.5 FM), WVFJ (93.3
FM).

Classical: WGKA (1190 AM), WABE (90.1 FM).

Diversified: WRAS (88.5 FM), WRFG (89.3
FM), WREK (91.1 FM).

Easy Listening: WPCH (94.9 FM).

Jazz: WCLK (91.9 FM).

MEDIA

News-talk: WDUN (550 AM), WGST (640 AM), WCNN (680 AM), WSB (750 AM).

Nostalgia: WQXI (790 AM), WLKQ (1460 AM).

Rhythm and blues: WIGO (1340 AM).

Rock: WKLS (96.1 FM), WAPW (99.7 FM).

Rock oldies: WFOX (97.1 AM), WLKQ (102.3 FM).

Urban Contemporary: WZGC (92.9 FM), WVEE (103.3 FM).

MOVIE THEATRES

Inside Perimeter:

AMC Galleria 8, Galleria Mall, I-285 & Hwy. 41, 952-0888

AMC Northlake Festival 8, Northlake Festival Shopping Center, La Vista Rd., Tucker, 934-7153

AMC Tower Place 6, Peachtree & Piedmont, 233-2151

Cinema 'n' Drafthouse, N. Druid Hills Rd. and I-85, 633-4011

Cineplex Odeon Marketsquare 4 at North Dekalb, 986-5050

Cineplex Odeon Phipps Plaza, 3500 Peachtree Rd., 986-5050

General Cinema Theatres Akers Mill Sq., Hwy. 41 N. near Cumberland Mall, 955-1795

General Cinema Theatres Northlake, I-285 exit at La Vista Rd. W., 934-7520

Hoyts Midtown, Promenade Center, 931 Monroe Dr., 872-6100

Hoyts Tara Cinema, Cheshire Bridge Rd. at I-85, 634-6288

Lefont Garden Hills, 2835 Peachtree Rd., 266-2202

Lefont Plaza Theatre, 1049 Ponce de Leon Ave., 873-1939

Lefont The Screening Room, 2581 Piedmont Rd., 231-1924

Northeast Plaza Cinema 12, 3365 Buford Hwy. N.E., 248-0624

Starlight Six Drive-In Theater, 2000 Moreland Ave. S.E., 627-5786

Storey No. 85 Twin Drive-In, I-85 at Shallowford, 451-4570

Storey 12 Oaks 4, Buford Hwy & Clairmont, 321-3601

Toco Hills, Toco Hills Promenade, 636-1858

United Artist CNN Cinema 6, CNN Center, 827-4000

United Artist Greenbriar, Greenbriar Mall, 344-8290

United Artist Lenox Square, Lenox Square Mall, 233-0338

United Artist South Dekalb, South Dekalb Mall, 241-6147

East:

Cineplex Odeon Mall Corners, 3650 Satellite Blvd., 986-5050

Cineplex Odeon Memorial 4, 6206 Memorial Dr., 986-5050

Cineplex Odeon Memorial 5, 5610 Memorial Dr., 986-5050

Cineplex Odeon Memorial Square, 5479 Memorial Dr., 986-5050

Cineplex Odeon Snellville, Hwy. 78 at Walton Ct., 986-5050

Cineplex Odeon Stonemont, 5241 Memorial Dr., 986-5050

Cineplex Odeon Stone Mountain Festival, Rockbridge Rd. at Hwy. 78, 986-5050

General Cinema Gwinnett Place, 1-85 & Pleasant Hill Rd., 476-0431

General Cinema Hairston 8 at Memorial Dr. and N. Hairston Rd., 879-6224

Litchfield, Covington and Panola Rds, 662-9889

Litchfield Peachtree Corners, 6135 Peachtree Pkwy., 662-9669

Litchfield Town Center, Across from Wal-Mart, Lawrenceville, 662-6220

United Artist Green's Corner, 4975 Jimmy Carter Blvd., 925-1376

United Artist Gwinnett, Gwinnett Mall, 623-1120

North:

AMC Cobb Place 8, Barrett Pkwy. off I-75, Kennesaw, 423-4837

Cineplex Odeon Brannon Square, 10675 Alpharetta Hwy., Roswell, 986-5050

Cineplex Odeon Friday's Plaza, 6285 Peachtree Industrial Blvd., Doraville, 458-4970

Cineplex Odeon Holcomb Woods, 1572 Holcomb Bridge Rd., 986-5050

Cineplex Odeon Merchants Exchange 5, 4400 Roswell Rd. and Rt. 120, 986-5050

Cineplex Odeon Promenade, 2400 Cobb Parkway, 986-5050

Cineplex Odeon Towne Center Village 6, Barrett Pkwy. at I-575, 986-5050

General Cinema, Merchants Walk, Johnson Ferry Rd. and SR 120, 971-1310

General Cinema Perimeter Mall, I-285 and Ashford-Dunwoody Rd., 394-4120

General Cinema Sandy Springs at Parkside, Sandy Springs Circle, Lower Level, 851-1890

Hoyts, Roswell Mall, Rt. 9 at Holcomb Bridge Rd., 998-1700

Litchfield, 1050 Powder Springs Rd., Marietta, 662-4224

Storey Town 8, Town Center at Cobb, 426-5400

United Artist Cobb Centre 6, 2120 South Cobb Dr. S.E., 436-1238

South:

Cineplex Odeon Southlake Festival 6, 1564 Southlake Pkwy., 986-5050

Cineplex Odeon Southlake 3, 1053 Morrow Industrial Blvd., 986-5050

Cineplex Odeon Westpark Walk Village, 500 Commerce Dr., 986-5050

Litchfield Rivergate, Hwy. 138 & Taylor, 662-6680

Litchfield Southlake, I-75 South at Hwy. 54, Morrow Industrial Blvd. exit, 961-8688

Storey National 7, I-285 & Old National Hwy., 762-9636, 436-1238

United Artist Cinemas 8 Southlake, Southlake Mall, 968-3119

West:

Cineplex Odeon Douglasville Cinema III, Fairburn Rd., 986-5050

Cineplex Odeon Douglasville Exchange, 7442 Douglas Blvd., 986-5050

Litchfield Austell Road, Austell Rd. at Floyd, Austell, 662-6224

Storey Shannon 7, Shannon Mall, 969-0606

United Artists Cinemas 8 Shannon, Shannon Mall, 964-3691, 436-1238

AROUND ATLANTA

For an interesting side trip within an hour or two of Atlanta:

Callaway Gardens. Take I-85 south to I-185 south, exit on U.S. Hwy. 27 south and continue into Pine Mountain, 404-663-2281. The 2500-acre garden includes a conservatory, the John A. Sibley Horticultural Center, the Day Butterfly Center, walking and biking trails and a beach complex.

Chateau Elan. Take I-85 north to exit 48 (Winder-Chestnut Mountain), 1-800-233-WINE. Tour the vineyards and winery; sample the prize-winning wine. You can dine in the chateau, visit the wine market and art gallery, and play golf on the 18-hole course.

Dahlonega. Take Ga. 400 north to Ga. 60, then north 5 miles to Dahlonega. (Chamber of Commerce, 404-864-3711.) A one-hour trip north to this historic town is guaranteed to produce fantasies about the gold-rush days. Gold was discovered here 20 years prior to the 1849 California gold rush.

Etowah Indian Mounds. Take I-75 north to Cartersville exit and follow the signs, 404-387-3747. In the lush Etowah River Valley once inhabited by native Americans, Indian relics dating between 1000 and 1500 A.D. have been excavated. Also on the site are undisturbed mounds and an interpretive museum.

Helen. Take I-85 north to I-985 to Gainesville, then U.S. 129 north to Ga. 75 into Helen. (Chamber of Commerce, 404-878-2521.) A charming Alpine-style village with Swiss chalets, interesting shops and cobblestone squares.

Madison. Take I-20 east 60 miles to Madison. (Chamber of Commerce, 404-342-4454; Madison-Morgan Cultural Center, 404-342-4743.) There are many beautiful antebellum homes in this town spared by Sherman on his march to the sea.

AROUND ATLANTA

Monastery of the Holy Ghost. Take I-20 east 30 miles to Covington; look for signs, 404-483-8705. In this Trappist abbey, the monks support the order by growing and selling plants and vegetables. The gift shop is filled with Christian artifacts and the famous, baked-on-site Monastery breads. Visitors are welcome on the grounds and to make overnight retreats.

Tanger Factory Outlet. Take I-85 north 65 miles to exit 53 on Hwy. 441, 404-335-4537. At the Commerce exit there is a something-for-everyone collection of factory outlet stores sure to please bargain-oriented shoppers.

Warm Springs. Take I-85 south to U.S. 27 Alternate, Moreland exit; turn left and follow route into Warm Springs. Franklin D. Roosevelt's cottage, the Little White House (where he died in 1945) is located here on Ga. 85. For information: 404-655-3511.